I0101033

British Birds

names ~ facts ~ myths

Geoff Green

Published by Geoff Green
Create Space

Copyright © 2015 Geoff Green

ISBN: 978-0-9933340-2-3

TABLE OF CONTENTS

PREFACE

This book explores the interesting and intriguing world of the meaning of and the stories behind the names of our British birds. The book aims to give readers an insight into how birds came to be given their names, the wide range of historical local names, the meaning of their formal (vernacular) English name and the derivation of their scientific names. It explores how much all this says about our long and intimate relationship with birds. The information provides a fascinating insight into the life, character and behaviour of birds and our response to and treatment of them. The book explores all three name categories for birds - local, vernacular(formal) and scientific names.

In addition the information on names is supplemented with interesting facts, data and insights about the individual bird to provide a fuller picture of the nature of the bird, often linked to the bird's name. Also included are some of the myths, tales, lore, stories and superstitions for many of our British birds which illustrates how important birds have been and are to us.

Throughout the book, where in a paragraph about a particular bird species there is some 'quite interesting' factual information given, you will see a large Qi symbol. This alerts the reader to facts which provide an interesting insight into the bird.

Enjoy this book as a serendipity of the fascinating meanings of the diverse names given to British birds, intriguing information on their lives and the many tales about them, true and otherwise.

This book covers a broad range of British birds (231 species in all) providing a detailed picture of the various aspects of many British birds and their   names.

WHAT'S IN A NAME?

When it comes to birds' names there is an enormous fund of fascinating information and meaning contained in the huge variety of names we have given to birds over the very long period of time that humans have been interacting with birds.

Human beings have lived with birds since time immemorial and integral to this they have been given a variety of names. These names reflect birds' behaviour, habits and characteristics along with all manner of beliefs, some of which are now enshrined in myths and folk lore. Birds feature in some of the oldest scripts and appear in very early art as well, such as cave drawings. An Aboriginal rock art depiction of a giant bird is possibly 40 000 years old. It is from this close attachment to birds and the relationship we have had with them for millennia that there is such a rich variety of birds' names. These names tell us a great deal about the birds themselves and our continuing close relationship with them. It also demonstrates how important birds have been in the everyday lives of people; how birds depend on us and are affected by our actions and often about our dependency on birds.

Some birds' names are derived from the call or song they make. Bird song has been an integral and important part of our lives for a long time. The formal English names of Curlew, Kittiwake and Cuckoo all represent their song in words, i.e. they are onomatopoeic. The common names for many birds are based on how people heard the bird's song and how they then sought to represent this sound in its name. So a common name for the Green Woodpecker is yaffler based on its distinctive call; a common name for the Bittern is boomer being a clear reference to that bird's deep boom and the Lapwing is still often called a peewit. The meaning of some words changes with time like the jar in the Nightjar's name which originally meant a quivering or grating sound rather than modern meaning of jar as discordant sound.

Birds' names are sometimes based on how they look. Many birds' names include reference to their colour, such as Blue Tit , Greenfinch and Goldfinch. Others refer to their appearance, like the Bullfinch, Common Crossbill and Short-eared Owl.

Other names refer to the bird's habitat, such as the Water Rail and Woodpigeon.

The derivation of some names is more obscure. Several birds' names are words that are not used in any other context e.g. Teal, Fulmar and Eider. Often the name derives from an older, dead language but at the time the name was given the word had an everyday meaning and reflected something relevant about the bird. Others are based on what is now proved to be a myth. For example,

Qi The **Wren**'s name derives from the word hen, based on the myth that the Wren was the hen to the cock Robin. Hence the rhyme "The Robin and Wren, are God Almighty's cock and hen". Clearly wrong but the name stuck! In the poem ' The death and burial of cock Robin' the Wren appears in 'Who'll bear the pall, 'We said the Wren', Both the cock and the hen, 'And we'll bear the pall'.

Finally, there are a number of birds which are named after famous people (often ornithologists) which must be the ultimate accolade for a birdwatcher! For example, Cetti's Warbler is named after the Italian mathematician and 18th century naturalist Fransesco Cetti.

All this illustrates how closely bound we have been to birds throughout history and remain so today. Birds are so much a part of our lives that their names tell us very rich and interesting tales. The rest of the book will examine this in a more detailed and structured way.

Before this a brief note on the three categories of birds' names:

Local and common names - those that have been used over time based on common usage. Many names were restricted to a locality, with some deriving from other countries. Several local names from Scotland are based on Norwegian or Icelandic names. In eastern and southern England names derived from France, Germany and the Netherlands. The total number of common and local names is not known as many have been lost over time, but the number is certainly large. The Wren alone has well over 40 recorded local names!

Formal English name - this is the unique name that has been designated by the British Ornithologists' Union (BOU) as the correct English vernacular name for each bird on the British list. The most recent list can be found at http://www.bou.org.uk/british-list/ . This name is the official name by which each bird should be referred to in Britain for the avoidance of doubt or confusion. Certainly historically there were several examples of confusion! There is good advice in the old Chinese proverb 'Wisdom begins with putting the right name on a thing'. The British Ornithologists' Union also acts as the body that decides which birds are on the British list. So if a new species of bird is spotted in Britain the evidence is scrutinised by the British Birds' Rarities Committee and its findings are ratified by the Union before the bird is placed on the British list. Currently (in 2012) there are 595 birds on the British list. The international formal English name given by the

International Ornithologists' Union can be differ from the BOU name. For example, the Bittern becomes the Eurasian Bittern and the Chaffinch becomes Common Chaffinch.

Scientific name - there is the internationally accepted method of giving each bird (and indeed all living organisms) a unique name using a binomial structure i.e. a name made up of two words. The words are usually Latin but some are Greek. Others are Latinised versions of words deriving from another language. Again the British list issued by the British Ornithologists' Union defines and publishes the unique, correct and agreed scientific name for each species of British bird. The list available from the web link above gives the scientific name for each bird on the British list. Matters get slightly more complicated when dealing with sub-species, but more of that later. This book includes 231 British birds but necessarily excludes vagrants and rarities. However, the choice is the author's own and these have been selected as ones of interest and for which relevant information is available.

LOCAL AND COMMON NAMES

From very early times, as humans and birds interacted with each other, a wide variety of names have been ascribed to birds. This has led to a plethora of local bird names, many of which have slid into antiquity and are no longer used. However, the record of these names tell us a great deal about our historical relationship with birds, including our use and abuse of them, our observation of their behaviour and names related to the sometimes super-natural powers that some birds were attributed with. Early references to birds include The Seafarer, dated pre-1000 AD in which the Swan (ylfete), Gull (maew), Eagle (earn) and Common Tern (stearn) are all mentioned. Chaucer, in his Parlement of Foules written in 1380, referred to the 35 species of bird who were used as a jury to select a bride for King Richard II.

Mixed in with this are some very strange tales, myths and folk lore. A few have stuck until the present day and influenced the official and accepted bird's name.

As each locality generated its own names for specific birds there are very many local variations. Attempts were made by people like Willughby and Ray in the 17th century to create lists of agreed names for birds but a variety of local names survived for a long time after this. This is not surprising as language was then predominantly an oral tradition and names would not transmit very far from the locality naming them. Also literacy levels were low and local dialects were predominant. These dialects generated bird names that would necessarily differ from other dialect names for the same bird. So local names persisted despite attempts to normalise them. In the 19th century scientists tried to compile a list of agreed birds' names which everyone would adopt but still common usage prevailed. This gave rise to confusion, particularly with respect to accurate bird identification, assigning birds to their correct family and identifying their near relatives. Hence some formal names are based on local names which are now known to be incorrect, for example the Wren already mentioned. Also some local names reflect the closeness of birds and humans by using human names for birds, for example jenny wren gives the Wren a female name.

Some local names have survived and a number became the formal English name for the bird or have been incorporated into the scientific name. This explains why some birds' names appear to be obscure and are not used in any other context.

The local names given to birds derived in a number of ways. Some came from the bird's colour, physical characteristics or behaviour. Others incorporated human names as a reflection of the closeness between birds and humans e.g. Jack, Madge and Gilly. Yet others came from the birds' environment. As bird observation was unrefined, the same bird name was used for several species, as a generic name e.g. willow wren and tit. Local names were also influenced by older names from abroad, typically from Scandinavia and continental Europe. For example, Scottish names were influenced by names from Scandinavia, the Shetlands by Iceland and S E England by Germany. Finally, various myths and folk tales were used to derive names. Below are examples from a range of birds that illustrate all these points. Local names are all written in lower case, even where the word might otherwise start with an upper case letter e.g. a human name. For ease of reference the birds are listed in alphabetical order of formal English name, rather than in strict taxonomic order. Also where there are several local names, they are listed in alphabetical order as well:

Qi One local name for the **Arctic Skua** was dung bird. This referred to the bird's habit of chasing and harassing other birds to provoke them to disgorge their food, which the Skua then eats. This behaviour is known as kleptoparasitism. Historically observers thought that the disgorge was dung, not food! The scientific name for the Arctic Skua is *Stercorarius parasiticus*. When translated *Stercorarius* means 'belonging to dung' and parasiticus means parasitic. So the bird has a scientific name which derives from a slightly incorrect observation of its behaviour. Other local names for the bird include Gaelic names like faskidar meaning squeezer and the Shetland name shooie, from the Old Norse tju (meaning thief) ; chaser; dirt bird and dung hunter, all of which reflect the bird's behaviour. The bird's nature is reflected in the North American name for this bird - Parasitic Jaeger, with Skuas being called Jaegers there. Jaeger is German for hunter.

The Arctic Skua's close cousin, the **Great Skua**, is called a bonxie to this day, which in Nordic means dumpy body. Other local names include dirten alan, as the bird acts like the Arctic Skua; herdsman, from the way the bird harried White-tailed Eagles away from lambs; morrel hen from its dark brown colouration; robber bird; tod bird, with tod meaning turd; tom harry from its habit of chasing other birds plus the use of human names for the bird and skooie. Britain is home to 50% of the world population of the Great Skua.

Qi The **Avocet** has many local names including cobbler's awl and shoe awl, which refers to its beak being shaped like an awl; crooked bill; scooper from its feeding action; and names like barker; clink and yelper from the sounds made by the bird when threatened. The Avocet became extinct in Britain in 1840. It returned to breed at Minsmere in

Suffolk in 1947, the unintended result of changes made during WW2 to the coastal defences which created an ideal environment for the bird to breed. The Avocet became the emblem of the Royal Society for the Protection of Birds. Numbers of breeding Avocet have increased over the last 25 years by about 500%, according to the Rare Breeding Birds Panel (reported in 2014). The bird's eggs are very pointed enabling the bird to arrange its normal clutch of 4 eggs close together so they are all warmed evenly by the adults' brood patch. Unlike other waders the Avocet has semi-webbed feet enabling it to paddle through water whilst feeding. The female's bill is longer than the males and is ideally shaped to turn the eggs in the nest to ensure they are evenly heated.

Qi The **Barn Owl** has been a familiar bird for centuries and humans have had a close relationship with it, not least because of its habit of nesting in buildings. The word Owl simply derives from howl, which is what this bird does with great gusto! If you get too near a Barn Owl it emits a screech that is truly frightening! The Barn Owl was given a large number of local names; up to 40. Many include human names such as billy whit; gill hooter; jenny owlet; madge moggy and padge (variation of Madge, from Margaret). Others include cherubim; church owl; death owl; demon owl; hobgoblin; monkey-faced owl; roarer; screech owl and white owl. All these various names reflect some observed aspect of the bird's behaviour or tales about the power of the bird. Some tales associated with the bird include its link to death. The myths and tales about Owls are detailed in the later Section 'Some common folk lore'. The first written record of the English name for the Barn Owl dates from the 10th century. Barn Owl numbers have increased by 270% over the last 25 years (Breeding Bird Survey in 2012). The oldest living Barn Owl recorded was 15 years old.

The Barn Owl is the most widespread bird in the world, being found on six of the seven continents. The Owl is an extremely skilful hunter, using its highly enhanced sense of hearing to locate prey. It is a specialised feeder, preferring Short-tailed Voles to any other rodent. The breeding success of the Barn Owl is directly correlated to the population of this Vole. The Owl has large asymmetric ears which are three times bigger than average for this size of bird. The ears work in stereo, which is why the bird moves its head from side to side, to get an aural positional fix on the location of its potential prey. The ears are set in the large facial disc, either side of its eyes, which acts as a reflector for the sound. The Barn Owl has 95 000 nerve cells in the auditory region of its brain compared to 27 000 in a Crow. Specially adapted feathers assist directing the sound into the ears and protect the ears from dust and injury. The basal membrane containing the sensory cells for hearing is 9mm long and contains 16 300 hair cells. The bird has the most sensitive hearing of any bird in the world. The owl also retains its acute hearing into old age because (unlike humans) the hairs that transmit the hearing signal to the brain regenerate to maintain their hearing. The Barn Owl is capable of catching prey in complete darkness (providing it has a mental visual map of its territory). Their flight feathers are specially adapted to be very quiet and emit sound at 1kHz which does not interfere with the sound emitted by their prey. Gilbert White in his famous book *The Natural History and Antiquities of Selborne* noted "the plumage of the remiges ... is remarkably soft and pliant. Perhaps it may be necessary that the wings of these birds should not make any resistance or rushing that they may be enabled to steal through the air unheard upon a nimble and watchful quarry". How right he was! The Barn Owl (along with other Owls and birds of prey) brood their eggs asynchronously. This means that as the eggs are laid they are brooded (mainly by the female). After about 48 hours they lay their next egg and brood this immediately. This leads to the first egg hatching first and the fledgling gets a head start over its siblings. When

11

food is in good supply all the hatchlings will fledge. However, in years of poor food supply the younger siblings will often die of starvation but the strategy means that at least the oldest chicks survive. For the Barn Owl this makes sense as they rely heavily on Short-tailed Field Voles, and the numbers of this species vary greatly from year to year.

Qi The **Bar-tailed Godwit** lives on mud-flats and is mainly a wintering bird, as the bird breeds in northern Scandinavia. Its local names included barwit; half curlew; prine; scammel; sea woodcock; set hammer; shrieker; speethe; stone plover and yarwhelp. Some names are shared with other, similar birds with the Avocet and Black-tailed Godwit also being called yarwhelp (from their call). Note the links to other birds, such as the Woodcock, Curlew and Plover, based on some common characteristic. Scammel comes from the bird's habit of sitting tight on its nest, and derives from the old word for limpet.

The Bar-tailed Godwit holds the world record for the longest known non-stop flight of any bird, flying from New Zealand to the Yellow Sea in China, a distance of 6,850 miles, taking 8 days. Another New Zealand bird flew 7,260 miles to Alaska. Like many birds the Godwit builds up huge fat reserves to make such a long flight. To make room for the fat and to keep its flying weight down it absorbs part of its tissues (like the liver and kidney) and then restores these to full functioning weight at the end of its flight. This process is known as auto cannibalism.

Qi The **Bittern** is a bird that is far more often heard than seen in its reed bed and bog environment and this is reflected in the many local

names given to the bird. The variety of names include bitter bump; bog trotter; boomer; bull o' the bog; bumble; clabitter and mire drum. It was once thought the bird made its booming call by thrusting its bill into the mud or pushing its bill into a reed and blowing. Tales such as these, albeit false ones, became established through the names given to the bird. In Suffolk a ship's fog-horn is called a sea bittern. Its low frequency voice (at 0.2 kHz) can be heard up to 3 km away.

Observers of the **Black Guillemot** (which is mainly seen in Scotland) noted the devotion of the sexes to each other and compared this to the similar behaviour of doves. This led to local Scottish names such as diving pigeon; dovekie; greenland dove; sea pigeon and sex turtle. In Orkney the bird was called tyst which derived from the Old Norse word peisti, based on the sound the bird makes. Other names include puffinet, comprised of puffin (which it resembles as a member of the auk family Alcidae) and the diminutive suffix –et; black puffin; spotted guillemot and turtur.

Qi The **Blackbird** is a well known British bird and has entered our culture through songs like the Beatle's Blackbird and the nursery rhyme "Four and twenty blackbirds baked in a pie". The latter sounds gruesome but in fact there was a practice of adding live birds to a pie just before serving, alarming guests when released. Local names

include black ouzel; blackie referring to its colour; colly; merle from the French for the bird and woosell, used by Shakespeare in Midsummer Night's Dream writing "the Woodsell cocke, so black of hue, with orange tawny bill". Ouzel is an old name for the bird and has now been utilised by the Blackbird's close relation the Ring Ouzel. The first written records in English for the Blackbird occurred in the 8th century. The Blackbird was the third most common bird recorded in the Garden Bird Survey in 2015. The Black bird was voted the Swedish national bird in 1962.

Qi The **Blackcap** has for a long time been a common summer visitor (and recently increasingly a winter migrant visitor). Blackcap numbers have increased by 270% over the last 40 years (Breeding Bird Survey in 2012). The bird has a very distinctive and beautiful song; some people

say it equals that of the Nightingale! Our forebears also thought so and they gave the bird names like mock nightingale and northern nightingale. Its other names derive from the bird's nesting materials hence the names black-headed hay-jack; hay bird; hay chat; jack straw and nettle creeper. As a bird that lives close to humans, other names came from human first names such as black-headed peggy and jack straw. Peggy was a word used for all warblers and jack denoted a small man, hence man of straw. Hay and straw refer to the bird's nesting material.

The Blackcap can be seen in Britain in winter, often visiting bird tables. These birds are likely to be Blackcaps from the continent, as our native birds migrate to North Africa. As with many small birds the Blackcap migrates at night to benefit from the cooler air, enabling them to conserve water. Their ideal air temperature for flying is 10 °C which can be attained at about 1000 m at night but requires a flying height of 3000 m during the day. The bird undertakes a full moult before migrating but it has to do this rapidly. Other birds, like its close relative the Garden Warbler, wait until they arrive at their winter quarters to moult. They also put on a great deal of weight in the form of fat which can be seen as fat globules on their chest when inspected. Oddly these birds (along with some other migratory birds) have a leapfrog pattern of migration, with the most northerly birds flying the furthest south i.e. the longest distance. In one experiment to determine if migration was a heritable characteristic, Blackcaps from the Canaries and Europe were inter-bred. The resulting hybrid offspring migrated to an intermediate area, proving that migratory instinct is inherited. The Blackcap is arriving 15 days earlier in Britain than 50 years ago as a result of climate change.

Qi The **Black-headed Gull** is a commonly occurring Gull and has an interesting range of local names. In previous centuries the bird was wholly coastal. Some names, like pick maw, include maw, which is a generic name for Gulls. Pick is from pitch, referring to the black head (in summer only, of course). Swabie, an Orkney name, has its origins in the Old Norse svarbakr via swart back (black back). Pewit gull is from its association with lapwings, which it still does today, with the Gull trying to steal food from the Lapwing. Another kleptoparasitic bird! In addition there are many other local names, given the bird's association with humans, including black hatto; carr swallow, with carr meaning pool; hoodie maa - a variation on maw meaning Gull; redshank gull; rittock; sea crow; sprat mew and tumbler. This bird was used as a substantial supply of meat and eggs. Commercial gulleries supplied up to 1000 eggs a day and into the 1940's Leadenhall market handled 300,000 of the bird's eggs in a year.

Qi The **Black-throated Diver** breeds in the far north of Scotland and Iceland. Its common name is loon, which means fool. Also its wailing cry is linked to lunacy, connecting loon with the modern word lunatic. There is also a connection to the moon, from the Latin *luna* alongside the lore that the full moon made people act crazily. Local names include herring bar; lesser imber; northern ducker and speckled loon.
  Immer comes from the Swedish for the grey ashes of a fire, referring to the bird's dark plumage or possibly from the Latin immergo - to immerse.

The bird is a consummately good swimmer and diver but on land it is clumsy, and its feet, through evolution, have moved towards its rear making it unstable on land. This has led to the name loon, which derives from the Swedish lom and the Old Dutch loen, all meaning clumsy through its inability to move fast when approached on land. The bird is one of the most ancient extant species of bird, with fossil records going back to the early Pleistocene period. In America the formal name for the bird is Pacific Loon.

In order to swim under water to catch fish, the bird has relatively short wings. They can dive to depths of 60 m which is helped by the fact their bones are heavy and solid, unlike most other birds that have a honeycombed, lighter bone structure. The down-side to having short wings is that in flight the smaller wings have to support a comparatively large body weight. Technically this leads to a high wing loading, measured as the weight supported per square centimetre of wing. As a primitive bird the Diver also has a high body density. A male diver weighs 3.4 kg and has a wing span of 120 cm. By comparison a Herring Gull weighs 1.2 kg and has a wing span of 144 cm, almost a third the weight and a larger wing area to support the weight. Hence divers need large lakes in order to take-off. A Diver can run for a ¼ mile before taking-off. Also they detect the direction of the head wind and fly into it for extra lift. Divers require large bodies of water to live on because on small bodies of water they would fail to get airborne. Also they need clear water to fish in as they feed by sight alone.

Qi The **Blue Tit** is a very common bird that associates itself with human habitation. In the RSPB Garden Bird Survey in 2014 the Blue Tit was the second most recorded bird (after the House Sparrow). Not surprisingly the bird has many local names, including billy biter; biting tom; blue bonnet; nun; pickatee; tinnock and titty mouse. Again, with a bird people have known for many centuries, some names include a

human name e.g. billy and tom. The word biter comes from the way the bird bites the fingers of those who interfere with its nest. Pickcheese is a Norfolk name from the habit of the bird pecking cheese. This is not far removed from the more recent habit this bird acquired of removing the foil top of bottles of milk left on door steps to get at the creamy milk! The first written record in English of the bird's name is from the 8th century.

As with many other birds, the Blue Tit can see the ultra-violet end of the light spectrum (as humans, we cannot). The male bird's blue cap emits ultra-violet light and this appears even brighter to the female and it attracts her to a suitable mate. Also the more yellow colour of the breast indicates that the male has eaten more caterpillars and so is likely to be a better provider for the female's off-spring. As a result of climate change the Blue Tit is breeding 10 days earlier than 40 years ago. The bird only lays one brood. Unusually, if the first brood is lost, there is no attempt to lay a second clutch, possibly because the caterpillar food for the young is no longer available.

The **Brent Goose** is a winter migrant from its breeding grounds on the Arctic coast of Siberia. Local names include brant, from which the formal name Brent derives via the Greek brenthos, for a water bird. The North American name for this bird is Brant. Other names include clatter goose; crocker; horra goose; hurrock, with hurr from its whining noise plus the -ock suffix; rott goose; routherock and ware goose, with ware the local Durham name for seaweed.

Qi The **Bullfinch** is another British bird that has been known to us for a long time. The bird is mentioned in the rhyme 'Who killed cock

Robin' as "Who'll toll the bell, I said the bull, because I can pull". Bull appears in the bird's formal name and refers to its thick neck. Local names also incorporate this such as bull spink, with spink being an old name for finch. Other local names include alp; bloor hoop; maple; mawpe and nope. Bud bird refers to the birds love of stripping fruit trees of their buds, much to the annoyance of fruit growers. The birds are selective and prefer Morello cherry trees and Conference pears (but not Hardy and Comice pears, which some fruit farmers grow to avoid predation by the bird). For this reason they were killed in large numbers, with a bounty of a penny a head in Elizabethan times. In Cheshire a bounty of 1p (old) was paid with 7000 killed in 36 years. After the 1954 Protection of Birds Act the Bullfinch could still be killed in fruit growing areas with a payment of £1 a bird. They will also eat buds from ornamental shrubs and ash keys. If their diet changes the birds lose their distinctive colours.

Bullfinch's mate for life and are both socially and sexually monogamous, the latter being unusual in birds. A pair remain together throughout the year, so when one is seen feeding the other will often be close by. The male bird emits a distinctive whistle which is a contact call, letting the female know where he is. When they meet again he will sometimes offer her some food. As there is no competition with rival males for the affection of a female the male has few sperm and no cloacal protuberance.

The **Buzzard** has in recent times become the most common bird of prey in Britain. Its numbers declined after the second world war as a result of the spread of myxomatosis in its rabbit prey. Gamekeepers also persecuted the bird. Since then numbers have recovered and the bird has spread to all areas of Britain with a 600% increase in numbers since 1967 (to 2008). Its local names include bald kite with a reference to the similar kite; barcutan; dancing hawk; gled; glider; pittle; putian meaning to push, thrust or swoop; puttock, from the Old English to swoop and shreak.

The **Carrion Crow** has been associated with humans for centuries and has many local names. These include black neb; crake being onomatopoeic; dowp; flesh crow from its reputation for eating dead flesh, like still born lambs; gore crow; ket crow with ket and gore being old words for carrion and land daw with daw being a generic word for the Crow family (as in Jackdaw). The Carrion Crow is disliked by farmers for harassing ewes and lambs and by gamekeepers for taking young game birds.

Qi Another bird that has for centuries been associated with human habitation is the **Chaffinch**. Over 40 local names have been recorded for this bird. A selection illustrating the wide variety includes apple bird; briskie; chink chawdy; dapfinch; pie finch; prink prink; sheld apple; tink; tree lintie and wet bird. Pie is used to denote coloured rather than the more recent meaning of black and white. Tink, chink and pink is onomatopoeic. Sheld means variegated (as in Shelduck). Wet bird is from the plaintive cry which was said to foretell rain. The first written record of the English name Chaffinch dates from 685 AD.

Like many Finches the bird was prized for its song and was kept as a caged bird. In full song the bird repeats its song phrase 6 times a minute and up to 300 times a day! In the 19th century birds that sang well were sold for 50 shillings and bird singing competitions were held. A report from Flanders records a song contest with a row of cages containing singing birds. The number of songs each bird sang was recorded and the winner was the bird that completed the most songs in 1 hour.

Some birds were cruelly blinded allegedly to make them sing better. Thomas Hardy wrote about this cruelty in his poem 'The blinded bird' writing ' So zestfully canst tough sing, And all this indignity, With God's consent, on thee, Blinded ere yet a wing, By the red-hot needle thou, I stand and wonder how, So zestfully though canst sing.'

 Experiments on Chaffinches demonstrated that birds are born with the ability to sing but learn the specific species' song from their parent. Birds reared in auditory isolation cannot sing the species' song. A castrated bird cannot sing but its ability to sing is restored when it's injected with testosterone.

The **Chiffchaff** is a common summer migrant and being known for centuries has many local names, including bank bottle and feather poke, both referring to its nest; chip chop; choice and cheep; least willow wren, when warblers were termed wrens and the Chiffchaff was seen correctly to be a close relative of the Willow Warbler; lesser pettychap; peggy, as another example of a bird acquiring a human name and wood oven.

Qi A bird that was more common in times past is the **Chough**. Currently it occurs in relatively low numbers in a few locations. It was formerly common in Cornwall, where it was kept as a pet. It has only recently returned as a breeding bird to that county. Local names include Cornish daw (daw from its call, same as Jackdaw) and cliff daw, referring to its habitat; fire raven - the Chough, Raven and Crow are all in the same Corvidae family; killigrew, from the Cornish village of the same name, market jew crow where market jew is an old name for Marazion (Cornish for market of Thursday), plus red-legged crow. The first written record of the English name Chough dates from the 10th century. The Chough appears on the Cornish coat of arms.

The **Common Sandpiper** breeds in some parts of upland Britain and is often seen as a migrant in autumn on its way to Africa to over-winter. Many of its local names refer to its shrill call, such as heather peeper; killy leepie; land laverock with latter word used for a Lark (which this bird is not!); otterling from the French otter meaning to shake or totter plus the suffix -ling; shore snipe and summer snipe (again the bird is not a Snipe either); tatler is from its voice; trillachan, which derives from the Gaelic meaning trill plus an -ach suffix and waterypleeps.

The **Common Tern** is a summer visitor to our shores. Several local names are based on its sharp, penetrating call, such as kirr mew (mew being an old word for Gull) and kipp. Its resemblance to a Swallow is reflected in the names sea swallow and shear tail. Other stranger names include darr; great purl; mirret; purre and sparling. The oldest living Common Tern recorded was 33 years old. Just how far this bird had flown we will never know, but it's a huge distance, given its annual migratory journeys to South Africa. Terns caught for their plumage for the millinery trade in the 19th century. The practice was made illegal 1922 under the Importation of Plumage (Prohibition) Act.

Qi The **Coot** is a common bird and is often found on lakes and even ponds so the bird has collected a few local names. These include bald coot (hence the expression 'as bald as a coot'); devil's bird from its blackness; pout, which derives from the French poult and the Latin pulla for chicken; queet, which is a Scottish word given to the Guillemot and white faced diver. Another phrase referring to the bird is 'crazy as a coot', associated with the way the birds squabble with each other. A rather odd tradition was the holding of a Coot Custard Fair in Norfolk in the 19th century. Sweet foods were made from eggs collected from Coots and Black-headed Gulls. Both birds were a common source of food at the time.

The **Cormorant** has long had a close association with coastal and island communities and so has many local names. The Liver bird associated with Liverpool is thought to be a Cormorant with two birds mounted prominently at the top of the Royal Liver Building. Local names include billy diver; coal goose, but it is not a goose; gor maw, with maw being a word for Gull, which it is not; hiblin from Old Norse reference to its white thigh patches; lairblade; mochrum eiders; parson from its appearance; scarf which imitates its croaking sound and sea hen, possibly from the fact its eggs were taken as food.

The jangling song of the **Corn Bunting** was formerly common in the British countryside. With changes to farming practices numbers have fallen by 81% in the last 25 years and is now extinct in Ireland (where it was once common). The Corn Bunting's local names include bunting lark; bush lark; common bunting; corn dumpling; ground lark; hirse lark; skitter brottie and thistle ock. The bird is highly promiscuous, with a record of one male mating with 18 females in one season!

The **Corncrake** was once a much more common bird than now. As a summer migrant it was thought the bird turned into a Water Rail in winter, so predictably the word rail appears in some of its local names, such as land rail. Other local names include corn scrack; crake gallinule, with gallinule a term for birds in the Rallidae family; creck from the sounds it makes and from which the scientific name *Crex crex* derives; daker hen; grass duck; king of the quail, as it takes off with flocks of migratory quail and meadow drake. The word rail comes from the French rale, a death rattle. The Corncrake's persistent call is loud, at 100dB, and the bird's ears have a reflex reaction to stop them being deafened by their own call! The bird's song is recalled in two poems - first 'The Landrail' by John Clare 'And still they hear the craiking sound, And still they wonder why, It surely cant be underground, Nor is it in the sky. An yet tis heard in every vale, An undiscovered song, And makes a pleasant wonder tale, For all the summer long.' and the second 'A voice of summer' by Norman MacCaig 'In this one of all fields, I know best, All day and night, hoarse and melodious, sounded A creeping Corncrake, coloured like the ground, Till the cats got him and gave the rough air rest.'

Qi The **Cuckoo** is an iconic and well-known bird not least because it is the only British bird that is wholly a brood parasite i.e. it always lays its eggs in the nest of another bird. Other British birds are partially brood parasites. Several spring plants are associated with the Cuckoo, such as Lady's smock which is called the cuckoo flower and Ragged robin flos-cuculi i.e. the cuckoo flower. Cuckoo spit is the froth that holds the froghopper bug. The plant Cuckoo pint derives its name from pint meaning penis. As it was not clear how the female Cuckoo mated the tale was that the phallic shaped flower of the Cuckoo pint flower served this purpose. Local names for the Cuckoo include geck; gowk, which is used to mean a simpleton; hobby, from its flight silhouette resembling a bird of prey and welsh ambassador. The term cuckold for a man with an unfaithful wife derives from this bird's behaviour of getting another bird to raise its young whilst the Cuckoo romped with the parasite's wife. Shakespeare referred to this in Love's labour lost "The cuckoo then in every tree Mocks married men, for thus sings he 'cuckoo'". The first English record of the name Cuckoo is from 650 AD.

The **Dipper** is found bobbing around on the water-side of streams and rivers looking for larvae to snatch from the water. Its local names incorporate names from the Thrush family (but it's not a member of the Turdidae family) like brook ousel; water blackbird and water ouzel. Others are bessy doucker, again a bird's name incorporating a human name; ess cock; water colly, dark as coal; water crake but the bird does not resemble a crake; water crow from its dark colour and water piet from the contrasting white breast with the rest of the body dark. Darwin studied the Dipper and noted the evolution of the bird to suit its watery environment. This includes dense feathers as insulation, enlarged oil glands to maintain the water-proofing of its feathers and a special nictitating membrane (third eye lid) to protect its eyes under water. It also has solid bones to help it submerge, whereas most bird have a honey-combed bone structure. The Dipper is the only British water song-bird. It also sings throughout the year to defend its territory. Experiments have shown that a higher quality of food given to fledglings led to these birds having a higher quality and more complex song when adults, which in turn led to higher reproduction rates.

The **Dunlin** is a winter migrant wader that visits Britain's estuaries in large numbers, with a small number breeding on our up-lands in summer. Local names include the diminutive jack, as in jack plover and jack snipe. Others names are churre, from its summer call; ebb sleeper; dorbie, a Scottish word for a small wader which pecks; ox bird, possibly from the black patch on the underside of the bird in breeding plumage; plover's page, from its association with Golden Plover on its breeding grounds and sea mouse, from its habit of scurrying around the fore shore.

Qi The **Dunnock** is a familiar bird to us in our gardens and countryside and has been so for generations. Its numbers have fluctuated in recent times, with a decrease of 30% over the last 40 years but a recovery of 21% in the last 25 years (Breeding Bird Survey in 2012). Not unsurprisingly it has acquired many names over time. Some of these include the word Sparrow, but this is an incorrect connection. Whilst the bird's colour resembles a Sparrow's, the bill is slender. This link led to the incorrect formal name of Hedge Sparrow which was changed in 1923 to Dunnock. The Old English name of hegesugge derives from hege for hedge and sugge for flutterer, a correct observation of the bird's habit of fluttering its wings, especially when breeding. Many names include hedge such as hedge creeper; hedge pick; hedge sparrow and hedge warbler, which is where it is seen. It also acquired human names such as issac, molly and philip. The bird was correctly identified as a host for the Cuckoo's egg hence the name blind dunnock, i.e. it does not see the Cuckoo laying an egg in its nest. The blue in blue sparrow; blue tom and blue dickie refers to the deep blue colour of the bird's eggs. This popular bird has over 45 local names! Shakespeare referred to the bird in King Lear - "The hedge sparrow fed the cuckoo so long, that it had its head bit off by its young".

Qi In areas where the **Gannet** breeds there is a close association with humans, not least as the bird was an important source of food. On St Kilda (now uninhabited) large numbers were caught and killed using a fowling rod to catch the bird. The birds provided vital food, feathers and skins. To give some idea of the magnitude of how many birds were caught Martin Martin recorded in 1698 'the number of Solan Geese consumed by each family the year before we came there amounted to twenty two thousand five hundred in the whole island, which they said was less then they ordinarily did, a great many being lost by the badness of the season'. A license is still issued for 2000 young to be caught for meat on Sula Sgeir (meaning Gannet skerry) by men from Lewis. Its name booby refers to the ease with which it caught. Bass goose and channel goose refer to the location of the bird, with the Bass Rock still a stronghold of the bird and has been from at least 1447. Albeit the bird is not a goose! Gannetries are occupied for centuries with records showing a colony on Lundy from 1274 until 1909. Solan goose derives from the crossed wing tips of the bird when sitting and sula is the Norwegian for Gannet. Mackerel gant is from its favourite food. Gannet is also slang for a greedy person e.g. 'to eat like a Gannet'. The first written record in English of the name Gannet dates from about 650 AD.

Qi The **Goldcrest** is Britain's smallest bird, being 8.5 cm long and weighing 6 g, the weight of a ten pence coin, half the weight of a Wren. Our resident population is supplemented in winter by migrants from Scandinavia. One local name is herring spink, from the habit of the bird

clinging to the rigging of fishing boats, plus tot o'er the seas, alluding to its migration. One belief was that this tiny bird would be incapable of flying across the Baltic and North seas so it hitched a ride on the back of the migrating Woodcock. Hence the Yorkshire name woodcock pilot. Swing tree is from the way the bird feeds upside down on branches. Other names associate the Goldcrest with the Wren with names like gold crested wren and golden cutty. Others refer to its diminutive size with names like thumb bird; tidley goldfinch (tidley meaning tiny) and wood titmouse (with titmouse previously being used as a general term for a small animal). The Goldcrest loses 20% of its weight in one cold night and has to eat constantly all day, consuming twice its body weight in food each day. The bird has three broods to maintain the population. The male looks after the first brood whilst the female moves to a new nest.

The **Goldeneye** is a distinctive winter migrant duck. Local names include freshwater wigeon; golden eyed garrot, from its distinctive white eye; gowdy duck; mussel cracker, except the duck is vegetarian; rattlewings, from the sound of its rapidly beating wings; whistler and whiteside.

Qi Another bird closely associated with humans is the **Goldfinch**. The bird has very many local names. Several relate to its bright colours, which made it attractive as a cage bird and its feathers for millinery use.

This practice was one of the first targets in the late 19th century for the recently formed Society for the Protection of Birds. Names include the ornate name, king harry, a reference to King Henry VIII's ornate clothing; lady with twelve flounces; proud tailor, from the white tips to its feathers; red cap - the bird has a red face rather than a red cap; seven coloured linnet and sheriff's man, from Shropshire referring to the black and yellow outfit of the sheriff. The bird is often seen eating thistle seeds so many names are based on this like thistle finch (which puts the bird in the correct Fringillidae family); thistle tweaker, from the Anglo Saxon thistletuige and thistle warp, from the way the bird deftly extracts the seeds. The Goldfinch has a high degree of coordination between its bill and feet enabling it to eat thistle seeds.

In the 19th century the birds were caught in a trap that is still used today (only under licence) called a chardonneret, being the French for Goldfinch. Then they were popular cage birds and there is a 19th century record from Worthing of 132 000 birds being caught. The Dutch painter Carel Fabritius painted a Goldfinch in captivity, held by a thin chain and shows the feeder from which the bird could be trained to draw water using a miniature bucket. The Dutch title for the painting is puttertje, meaning little weller. This explains the British local names of draw water and draw bird.

The **Great Black-backed Gull** is the world's largest Gull, weighing 1700 g compared to the Herring Gull's 1200 g. One local name was goose gull with this Gull weighing more than the Brent Goose. Other names include baakie from its cry; black back; carrion gull; parson gull; saddle back; swaabie and wagel is a Cornish name for the immature bird, once thought to be a separate species.

Qi The **Great Grey Shrike** has a number of striking local names, linked to its gruesome habit of catching its insect prey and impaling them on a spike or thorn to ensure they do not escape before being eaten. Hence the names butcher bird and murdering bird. Shrike probably derives from the Old English scric representing the bird's shrieking cry (this name is also used for the Mistle Thrush for the same reason). The local name nine killer comes from the myth that the Shrike killed nine birds a day. The ornate name white whiskey john refers to the bird's white under parts, revealed as it flicks its tail from side to side. The bird has exceptionally good eyesight and the Shrike was used by trappers to alert them to an approaching bird from a great distance, with the Shrike also indicating the direction of the incoming bird's flight.

The **Great Northern Diver** breeds in northern Scotland and shares the common name of loon with the Black-necked Diver (see above). Its other local names include arran hawk; bishop from its distinctive neck pattern; ember goose; great doucker and immer diver. Immer derives from the Latin immergo, to immerse. The Icelandic name for the bird is himbrimi.

Qi The **Great Tit** has a range of interesting local names. Titmouse incorporates tit, which was a name for any small creature and mouse as a term for the tit family. Ox eye derives from the French for a small animal. The names black-headed bob, joe ben and tom noup, illustrate a bird acquiring a man's first name. Other names are carpenter bird; sawfinch and saw sharpener, all referring to the sound made by the male in the breeding season.

The Great Tit alters its diet in winter, eating Beech mast. To do this the bird's bill changes shape to a deeper, shorter shape. In summer the bill is thinner for eating insects. Research has shown that UK Great Tits use bird feeders more frequently than Dutch birds and as a result their bills are slightly longer. Also UK Great Tits have a higher fledgling rate (live chicks surviving) than its Dutch relatives. The Great Tit incubates eggs for varying lengths of time per day depending on weather. On warmer days the female incubates for a longer period, so that her eggs hatch sooner to align with the earlier emergence of the moth caterpillars they rely on. The caterpillars are only available for 2 weeks so the bird needs accurate timing to breed successfully. The Great Tit has a loud song and, much to many a birdwatcher's irritation, it has a highly varied song. In urban areas its song is louder and higher pitched to be better heard by overcoming background noise. However, males which sing a lower note are better at attracting females and those that have a more extensive song repertoire can defend a larger territory. Also the strength of the male's breast colour varies, with a brighter colour being more attractive to females. Great Tit numbers have increased over the last 40 years (to 2012) by 88%.

Qi A bird recorded in Roman mythology and which has been well known to the British for a long time is the **Green Woodpecker.** The bird is associated with rain and has names like rain bird; wet bird; weathercock and whetile, from wet tail. It also has a distinctive call which is still referred to as a yaffle, hence yafflingale; laughing bird and yaffler. It lives in trees, although it frequently feeds on the ground, leading to names like wood fucker, with fucker originating from the Dutch fokken meaning to knock (only more recently has the word become obscene); wood hack; wood pie; wood speck and wood sucker. Popinjay has been used as name, which is an early name for parrot (due to the similar colouring). The number of Green Woodpeckers has doubled over the last 40 years (to 2012).

Like many of the Woodpecker family (Picidae) the Green Woodpecker has a very long tongue which it uses to find and consume its prey (typically ants). The tongue has small hooks at the end to catch its insect prey. The long tongue retracts back through the mouth and coils up in the cranium. The Green Woodpecker in fact rarely drums like its close relatives the Great and Lesser Spotted Woodpeckers. It does however excavate a hole in a tree for its nest. Also it feeds mainly on the ground. The Green Woodpecker (also like its cousins) has a zygodactyl arrangement of its toes, with the second and third pointing to the front and the first and fourth toes to the rear, which assists the bird in holding vertically onto the side of a tree. (NB. birds only have four toes or fewer). Also its tail feathers are strengthened so the tail is used in conjunction with its legs to hold the bird vertically on the side of a tree.

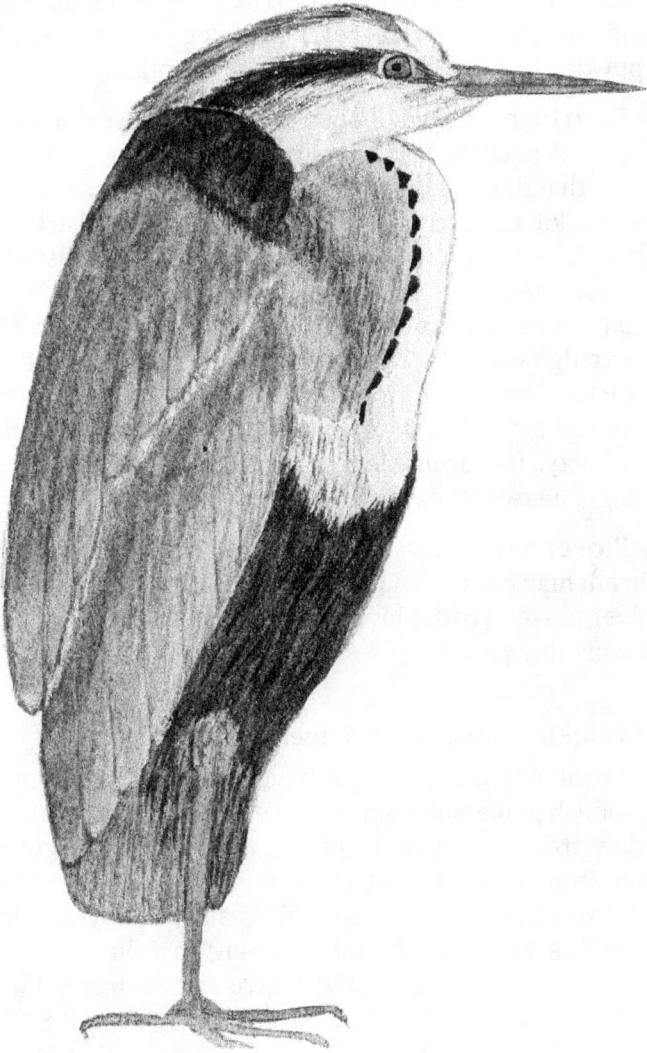

Grey Heron

The **Grey Heron** has been well known for centuries and is seen throughout Britain. Some of its local names are from human names such as frank from its call; jack heron (for the male); jenny crow; joan-na-ma-crank and moll heron (for the female). Shitepoke comes from the bird's habit of defecating when flushed and shiterow, which was also a derogatory term for a thin, weak person. Other names include hegrie; hernshaw as a name for a young heron; lang-leggity beastie; longie crane and long-necked longnix. The Grey Heron does not have a preen gland (which produces a water-proofing oil) like many birds but uses the powder from its feathers for water proofing.

The **Grey Partridge** is a bird of open farmland whose numbers have declined by 79% over the last 25 years (to 2011) largely due to the use of herbicides that destroy the weeds the adult bird feeds on and pesticides that kill the insects the young feed on. It is also bred for sport and is easy to shoot as it flies but short distances when disturbed and keeps to a restricted area. Local names include brown partridge; girigrick; patrig; pertriche and stumpey. Its close cousin, the **Red-legged Partridge** was introduced from France in the 17th century. Not surprisingly local names for this bird include frenchman. It is less favoured as a game bird as the bird tends to run rather than fly and its meat is less tasty. It is probable that the partridge in the pear tree of the famous song 'The twelve days of Christmas' is this bird.

The **Grey Plover** has a diverse range of local names including bull head; chuckly-head; may cock; mud plover; owl head; ox-eye; sea cock; sea plover; silver plover; (with plover inexplicably associating the bird with rain) and whistling plover.

Qi The **Guillemot** breeds in summer on precipitous rock faces and spends the winter at sea. The Scots have given the bird many names including foolish guillemot from the ease with which it is caught for food; kiddaw, from the call of the young; marrot, from its gutteral call; queet, a variation on coot; scoot and willock from the call of the juvenile. The adult birds can recognise the specific call of their young in amongst the very close packed, noisy colonies nesting on a cliff. Shuttock refers to the very dirty mess of the colony. Murre derives from its gruff call and is the American name for the bird and the Guillemot family.

Guillemot

Guillemot eggs have adapted into a pyriform, tapered shape. Traditionally this was thought to be based on the idea that if the egg is disturbed on the very narrow ledges the birds nest on, it will spin round but not fall off and smash. However research has shown that this shape does not particularly help keep the egg on its narrow nest. It is in fact a shape that minimises the effect of impacts as the birds alight on the nest ledge. The shape also ensures that the egg and chick is less contaminated by the considerable amount of faecal material that litters the ledge. The markings on and colours of the eggs vary more than any other bird in the world. This prevents confusion between the birds on the owners hip of eggs on the tightly packed, highly populated cliff colonies – where there are up to 70 pairs/m². A triumph of avian artistry! Each egg weighs about 100 g, the equivalent of a woman giving birth to a 12 kg baby! The eggs are very nutritional and were collected in large numbers. One record for one day in one place shows 6800 eggs were collected.

Guillemots catch fish head first, lengthways in their bill. The head is first pre-digested in the adult's throat then the fish is turned around and presented to the hungry chick.

Guillemots were taken on St Kilda by lowering a man to rock face where he stayed all night. The birds were caught as they returned at dawn, using a white handkerchief to lure the birds and catching them when they alighted. Adults were caught early in the season when they were fat and palatable. Up to seventy birds were caught this way by one man in one night. The birds were shot for food and this led to the extinction of the bird in certain areas such as Beachy Head in Sussex. A report in 1868 reported that 168 000 birds were shot by pleasure parties over a 4 month period. The Guillemot is a consummate diver and can reach depths of 180 m.

The juvenile birds, called jumplings, leave their ledge nest when only about two thirds fully grown (at about 18/25 days old), and with their wings not fully formed. The young birds jump off the cliffs at night (assisted by parents) and the father joins the juvenile and together they swim off to Norway, the juvenile bird maturing as it goes. This strategy has been proved to be based on the fact that the father can catch more food for the juvenile whilst swimming at sea rather than make long, arduous journeys to feeding grounds and back to the cliff nest. By October it is fully grown and can then migrate. The birds do not fly far away e.g. to the Bay of Biscay before returning to their breeding colonies.

The **Hen Harrier**'s identification was unclear for many centuries due to confusion with Montagu's Harrier. Many local names refer to the bird's colour, like blue gled (gled is a name used generally for hawks); blue hawk; grey buzzard; white aboon gled and white hawk. Ring tail is still used to refer to the female's distinctive white tail band which mis-led observers to think it was a different species from the lighter coloured male. Furze hawk; gorse hawk and moor hawk all refer to the bird's environment. Flapper is from its slow wing beat flight.

The **House Sparrow** was formerly common and closely associated with human dwellings. However, numbers have decreased by 71% over the 40 years (to 2009). It has now reached top spot in the Garden Birdwatch survey (2015). Its various local names include craff; cuddy, also used for the Dunnock (which was erroneously called a Sparrow for a long time); easing sparrow, from nesting in eaves; spadger from the Old English spara; squidgie and thack sparrow from thatch.

Qi The **Jay** can be seen and heard in woodlands, particularly in autumn as it gathers acorns. Some local names refer to the bright turquoise colour on its wings, such as blue jay. The bird also has human name connection through jenny jay and references to its noisy nature in devel scritch and scold. Oak jackdaw associates the bird correctly with oak woodland. A Jay can hide up to 5000 acorns and is a key species in the regeneration of oak woodland, as the bird fails to retrieve all its buried treasure. Retrieval rates have been monitored and vary between 30 and 75%. The Jay buries its cache anywhere and helps woodland spread up-hill as acorns naturally only fall beneath or lower than the tree, not higher. In a German study each bird stored about 4500 acorns, carried them up to 4km away and travelled 175km per day.

The word jay is used to describe a foolish person or those who chatter loudly. American slang uses jay as a person who chatters impertinently. Jaywalking is a term used to describe someone who carelessly crosses the street.

Qi The **Kestrel** is often seen hovering and several of its local names come from this habit, like hover hawk; fanner hawk; fuckwind, with the first syllable not originally being an obscenity but meaning to beat or fan; hover hawk; wind bibber; wind fanner and wind hover. In Sussex the name wind bibber derived from the local word bibber meaning to shake. The Kestrel is now established as a Falcon (the family Falconidae) and not a Hawk (the family Accipitridae), but the two families are closely related. The name cress hawk comes from the

French creselle, to rattle, referring to the bird's courtship call, as does the name keelie. The name stanniel means stone yeller, from the bird's habit of calling from rocks. The Kestrel is the lowest bird in the falconry hierarchy and is flown by a knave. As a demonstration of how birds are still ingrained into our culture, the Kestrel was central to the famous 1969 film Kes, based on a novel entitled 'A Kestrel for a knave'. In the film a down trodden boy finds redemption by establishing a relationship with a Kestrel.

Kestrel

As mentioned in the paragraph on the Blue Tit, birds can see in the ultra-violet range of the light spectrum. The Kestrel utilises this to catch its favourite prey, the Field Vole. As the rodent runs it urinates and this emits ultra-violet light, which the bird sees and uses to locate its prey. The Kestrel is the only British bird of prey to systematically hover and is able to keep it eye almost motionless as it beats its wings into the wind. When hovering the bird's eye hardly moves (max. 6mm) and it does this by moving its head back and forth to conserve energy by gliding for a short time rather than flapping all the time. Technically the bird does not hover by remaining stationery like a hummingbird, but it flies into the wind to balance itself. The bird can only hover for 3.5 hours a day to balance energy gain and expenditure. Hovering is a high energy activity but it pays off for the Kestrel, which needs at least 4 Voles (or similar animal) per day increasing to 8 a day whilst breeding. Kestrel numbers have fallen over the last 15 years by 35%.

The **Kittiwake** is another coastal bird that we have known for centuries and has plenty of local names. The Kittiwake is the only British gull that is truly pelagic, spending all its non-breeding time at sea. The bird and its eggs were a source of food. Several of the names are redundant words like annet; reddag; rippack ritto; rittock and weeo. Many of these names are from north Scotland where the bird nests in large numbers and was caught for food. Tarrock is a Cornish word for the juvenile, and its bold black and white colouration led observers to think the juvenile was a separate species. Some names refer to Gulls, such as haddock gull; jack gull and snow gull. The bird is a member of the Gull family, Laridae and is the only British gull that is a true sea bird, others are merely coastal.

Qi Another bird with a myriad local names is the **Lapwing**, a bird well known on the coast and inland throughout Britain. As the bird has been known for many centuries some local names derive from Old and Middle English plus many regional variations. Peewit, which is onomatopoeic, is still used today. Others include flap jack and flop wing, both from its distinctive flight; green plover, derived from the Old French word plouvier, related to its far reaching call; horn pie, from its colouration (pied historically meant coloured rather than the modern black and white) and horny wick, from its crest. The name Plover has an unclear association with rain, deriving from the Latin pluvia meaning to rain. Lymptwigg is an Exmoor name, from the parent bird's habit of feigning a broken wing to distract predators from their young. The local

Lincolnshire name for the Lapwing was pyewipe and there is a place with this name near Grimsby.

The Lapwing's eggs were taken as food and the bird was also eaten in large numbers. A record from Thetford states 3,360 eggs were taken in one year. One operator recorded taking 6-700 eggs a week and in 1820 they sold for 3/- (now 15 p) a dozen. Oddly the Lapwing changes its feeding habits 2 to 3 days either side of a full moon. During this period the birds feed throughout the night and roost and sleep during the day. This behaviour is not understood! Numbers of breeding birds have fallen by 64% over the last 40 years (to 2012).

Another member of the Finch family (Fringillidae) that sings well, the **Linnet**, was previously caught and kept as a cage bird. Several names refer to the male's red crown and chest like blood linnet and red headed finch with brown linnet; grey linnet; thorn grey and whin grey all referring to its winter colours plus the odd name lemon bird. Furze linnet; gorse linnet and heather linnet all refer to its environment. The name Linnet appears in the song 'My old man' recalling that 'off went the van with my home packed in it, I followed with my old cock Linnet.....'

The **Little Grebe** is Britain's smallest Grebe and is found on reed fringed pools and lakes. It readily dives to feed and to escape any perceived danger. Local names refer to its habit of diving like divedop and doucker, a name used for a diverse range of birds such as the Common Scoter, Dipper, Goldeneye, Great Northern Diver and the Tufted Duck. A rather eclectic mixture, except they are all water birds. The common name dabchick is still used by bird watchers. Dabchick derives from the Middle English dobchick, with doppe being a diving bird.

The **Long-tailed Duck** is seen around our shores in winter after breeding on the Arctic coasts of North America, Europe and Russia. The bird has acquired a number of descriptive local names such as calloo from its call; coal and candlelight, alluding to its black and white colouring; hound duck; old squaw; sea pheasant; sharp tailed duck and swallow tailed sheldrake referring to the male's long, thin tail, with sheld meaning varigated.

Qi The **Long-tailed Tit** is often seen and heard in flocks that move quickly from tree to tree. The bird has many local names including bag;

barrel tit; bottle jug; creak mouse; feather poke; jack-in-a-bottle referring to its nest; long pod; juggy wren with wren a name often used for small birds; long tailed chitterling; poke pudding; ragamuffin and rose muffin from its colouration. The bird's nest is a marvel of avian engineering. Up to 2000 feathers are used in its construction along with moss, lichen and spider's web to bind it all together. The nest is dome shaped to keep predators out and the occupants warm. The nest hangs from a suitable branch and is designed to expand as the fledglings grow. Unusually amongst birds, if a pair's nest fails the birds will then assist other pairs to raise their young.

A member of the Crow family Corvidae that is a familiar sight and sound is the **Magpie**. The bird has an interesting range of local names like chatter pie; haggess; maggett, from its habit of probing carrion for maggots; miggie; mock-a-pie; nanpie and tell pie. Pie occurs frequently in bird's names and was originally used to denote a bird with a mixture of colours where now pie or pied is used for a mix of black and white. Haggess derives from the French agace, denoting a sharp, pointed tail, similar to the Cornish name cornish pheasant.

Qi The **Marsh Harrier** is true to its name and breeds in marshes. Up to the 17th century the birds was common in East Anglia. Numbers fell rapidly when the fens were drained. Then as a predatory bird it was heavily persecuted and almost driven to extinction in Britain in the 19th century. By the turn of the 20th century there were no records of the bird breeding. As numbers recovered from the mid 1920's, the Harrier was affected by the organochloride chemicals that affected many birds of prey (see under Sparrowhawk Page XX). Local names include bald buzzard; bog gled; duck hawk; dun pickle, with dun from the duller colour of the female and pickle from pittle (an old word for Buzzard); moor buzzard; red harrier, referring to the brighter coloured male bird; snipe hawk and white headed harpy, with harpy being a bird of prey with a woman's face and more recently meaning a woman who draws a man into her grasp. A photograph of the Marsh Harrier (taken by the famous Eric Hosking) was adopted as its insignia by an RAF platoon. The name Harrier was also used by the RAF for the innovative vertical take-off aircraft in the 1960's.

The male bird transfers food to its mate using an aerial pass. He calls to the female who leaves her nest and flies to meet the male who drops the food for the female to accurately catch in her talons. This eliminates the need for the more colourful male to go near the nest and thus reduces the risk of ground predators finding the nest. Often the female chooses an older male, even if the male already has several mates, as they are better hunters and provide more food than a young inexperienced male would. The birds have very good hearing, possessing large ears (almost the size of an Owl's) but unlike the Owls, they do not have stereo hearing i.e. the ears are placed symmetrically on their face. Combined with good eye sight the birds are highly efficient hunters.

A bird frequently seen on open land and moors is the **Meadow Pipit.** It is frequently used by the Cuckoo as a host species, which was accurately observed in times past, hence the names cuckoo's sandling; cuckoo's titling and gowk's fool. Some of its other names include earth titling; meadow titling and tit lark, the word tit denoting a small animal; moor peep and pipit lark associating the bird with other species (Larks do look very similar). Another set of names associate the bird with its environment such as heather lintie; ling bird; moor titling and moss cheeper.

Thrushes have been closely linked to humans for centuries and the **Mistle Thrush** is no exception. Over 40 local names have been recorded for this bird. Many refer to its song and call such as horse thrush, where the cry is said to sound like a horse neighing; rattle thrush; screech thrush from its alarm call; shrill cock and squawking thrush. Hollin cock refers to the habit of feeding on holly, as does holm screech. Norman gizer comes from its aggressive behaviour and gizer from the French for mistletoe. Storm cock refers to the fact that the bird continues to sing during a storm. Finally jeremy joy uses a man's first name and reflects the way the bird sings in January, as one of our early songsters. Throstle is a traditional name used for the thrush family and links to the Old English prostle and the German drostel.

The **Nightjar** has been known to us for centuries and in the 16th century was known as 'birdes that in the night sucke goats'. This tale is explored later in the section below. Local names include churn owl; fern owl and jar owl referring to its heath land habitat; night churr; night crow; night hawk and night swallow all refer to the bird's nocturnal habits but with little agreement on who its close relatives are! Other names are the amusing name flying toad; goat owl; lich fowl, which associates the bird with death and puckeridge which is a disease in cattle that the bird was allegedly responsible for. One belief was that the calls of the Nightjar were the sound of witches hiding in the bushes.

Qi The **Nuthatch** is a bird of woodland and its feeding habits form the basis for many of its local names, like nut jobber, where job is an old verb meaning to peck or jab; nuthack and woodcracker from its habit of tapping trees for insects. Mud dauber and mud stopper derive from how the bird uses mud to stop up its tree nesting hole. The name jar bird was used by Gilbert White, of Selbourne fame, from the sound made whilst hacking. The Nuthatch is the only British bird that can climb down a tree. In fact members of the Nuthatch family are the only birds in the world that can climb down a tree. Nuthatch numbers have increased by 250% over the last 40 years (Breeding Bird Survey in 2012).

Qi A familiar sight and sound on estuaries and mud flats is the **Oystercatcher**. This distinctive bird's names include chalder; mere pie deriving from its variegated plumage; mussel cracker, with mussels (rather than oysters) being one of its foods of choice in Britain; sea nanpie; sea pie and trillachan, a St Kildan name, with trill referring to its shrill call and the suffix –ach. Other names are dickie bird; oyster plover; scolder; sea pynot and shalder. The British bird does not eat oysters (but continental birds do). The Oystercatcher can eat up to 500 cockles a day, about 40% of its own body weight, about 180 lbs. in a year! In the 1960's the bird was culled to reduce the loss of cockles on commercial beds, but this had no effect on the number of cockles! The shape of the tip of the bill varies depending on the seafood it eats and the manner in which it opens the shells. Some are chisel shaped and others more pointed. The shape varies with the season and the availability of certain food. The oldest living Oystercatcher recorded was 40 years 1 month old.

Peregrine

Qi As the fastest animal on earth, (reaching up to 200 mph in vertical stoop flight) the **Peregrine** was the falconers' choice of falcon and the male could only be flown by an earl and the female by a duke. Only the Gyr Falcon and Golden Eagle rank higher in falconry. Needless to say the bird has several local names, mainly linked to its status as a hunting bird. Many names use the word hawk, allocated before the difference between hawk and falcon was established. Names include blue hawk; cliff hawk, where it often seen; duck hawk; haggard falcon; passenger falcon; perry hawk; pigeon hawk, from its prey and spotted hawk. Tiercel gentle is the name given to the male (and to some other male birds of prey) from the French la tierce, meaning a third, which refers to the proportionately smaller size of the male. It is common amongst birds of prey for the male to be considerably smaller than the female. The male weighs about 670 g and the female 1100 g. Falconers kept moulting birds in cages called a mew, being an old word for a moulting falcon. This word is now used for a small building at the back of a house. The Peregrine's feathers are not fully water proofed so the bird rarely takes its prey in water, preferring to take prey in the air. The Peregrine is the fastest animal in the world, reaching speeds of nearly 300 km/hr in a stoop flight and experiences an 18 g force . The diving bird doesn't just follow its prey, it intercepts its line of flight, like a military missile. The tendons in its feet have a ratchet mechanism that locks its talons onto its prey. Its eyes occupy 50% of its skull (compared to 5% for humans) and the retina has two fovea, one for distance vision and one for close vision. To ensure that its lungs do not burst whilst flying at such a high speed, the nostrils have cones to enable the bird to carry on breathing. This design was adapted by aeronautical engineers who fitted cones to the front of jet engines to reduce the effect of turbulence created at high speed, without which the engines would fail to work.

Female Peregrine's, weighing on average 1140 g, are capable of catching and killing a Great Black-backed Gull weighing 1350 g and cock Black Grouse weighing 1300 g. Records show that in the UK the total number of species caught by the Peregrine is 132 and from records in Europe the total is 210. However, the majority of its prey are Rock Doves and its close relative the carrier and homing pigeons, much to the annoyance of pigeon breeders. Based on data from observations the estimated annual consumption of food by a family of Peregrines is 224 kg.

The **Pied Wagtail** is a familiar bird in towns and in the countryside and is easy to identify from its name - a black and white bird that wags its tail! The word pied has recently taken on the meaning of black and white (as in this case) where it used to mean coloured. Local names include dishwasher and links the bird to puddles created by washing; dishwipe; lady wagtail; polly washdish; waggie; wagging tale; wagstart, with start being an old word for tail; washtail and white wagtail a name now given to the continental species of this bird. Pied Wagtails form noisy large roosts of up to 4000 birds in winter and it not uncommon for roosts to form in town and city centres.

The **Pochard** breeds in small numbers in Britain but numbers are supplemented in winter by continental birds. Often only males are seen as the females leave the males and migrate further south. Local names include blue poker; poker and red-headed poker, from its feeding habit. Other names include fresh water wigeon; red-headed curre; red-headed wigeon and well plum.

The **Puffin** is an iconic bird, mainly because of its large and colourful bill (the distinctive colours are acquired just for the summer). The bird bred in large numbers on cliffs around our coast and was an important source of food in some areas. Names given to the Puffin often refer to its bill or large belly, such as bouger, from the Norwegian for belly; bulker, from the Gaelic bulgair for bird with belly; coulter neb, coulter is Northumbrian word for plough share and neb an old name for nose; norie, used in Orkney deriving from the Icelandic nori, for something chipped off; pope, a derogatory reference to its nose and tammie norie referring to a shy person. The name of Lundy Island, in the Bristol Channel comes from the Old Norse lund, meaning Puffin. Puffins were once caught in large numbers, with one estimate of 90 000 birds a year taken. The bird was caught using a fleyging, which is a 12 foot pole with

a net to catch the birds in flight. The birds were boiled or smoked and the feathers used as down. This was often women's work with women left on remote islands for 3 weeks at a time to collect birds for their feathers. On St Kilda more Puffins were killed than any other bird. In 1876 89,000 were killed, with 4,800 lbs of feathers taken in 1894 from 90,000 birds. The Puffin was declared fish meat by the church and could be eaten during Lent. The oldest living Puffin recorded was 35 years 11 months old.

The Puffin is often seen photographed with several sand eels in its beak. It manages to retain its catch whilst continuing to fish because its beak is hinged so that the mandibles remain parallel. The young leave the nest on their own and have to work out a migration route for themselves, unaided by either parent. On leaving the breeding colony the adults fly off on separate migration routes and spend the winter wholly at sea. Little is known about exactly where Puffins spend winter as they disperse over a wide area. In winter the beak colouring disappears and returns ready for the next year's breeding season. In spring the adults return to the same breeding colony and re-establish their pairing with a flamboyant display, involving their colourful beak.

The **Quail** has been known since biblical times when the Israelites were twice given them as food whilst in the desert after fleeing from Egypt (see Exodus 16:13). The bird in fact does migrate through Israel. In Britain it is heard more often than seen as it skulks, calling in long grass. The Quail's local names refer to its call which is similar to the Corncrake (no relation) and wet-me-lip. Other names include bobwhite; but-for-but; fey fool; quick-me-dick and throsher. The bird was killed in large numbers, luring them using pipes replicating the bird's call. The Quail has a very short breeding cycle and young birds can breed aged only 12 weeks. This enables the bird to breed during its migratory journey, with the young continuing the journey, in a similar manner to some butterflies.

The fortunes of the **Red Kite** have fluctuated wildly. In the Middle Ages the bird was numerous, especially in cities where it was an effective scavenger. The birds was extinct in England by 1870 and in Scotland by 1900 as a result of improved sanitation and refuse disposal, plus the destructive actions of gamekeepers, and egg and skin collectors. In the 20th century the bird faced extinction with just a few birds remaining in Wales. Myxomatosis and the use of the sheep dip dieldrin adversely affected the few remaining birds. By the early 1980's it was a globally threatened species. A successful re-introduction programme was started in 1989 in Scotland and Buckinghamshire leading to wild birds breeding by 1994. Numbers have increased rapidly and the bird is now colonising other areas of Britain. Local names include bald kite; crotch tail from its distinctive forked tail; gled meaning glider and puttock meaning swooper, which is also a name for the Buzzard and the Harriers.

The **Redshank**'s piping call is redolent of walks around marshes and estuaries in winter. Whilst still common numbers have fallen by 69% in the last 34 years to 2011. Local names include pool snipe; red-legged horseman; warden of the marshes; watery peeps and yelper.

Not unsurprisingly local names for the **Redstart** focus on the bird's bright red tail, found on both sexes. These names include bessy brantail; brand tail, as in fire brand; fanny redtail; fire flirt, from the movement of its tail; fire tail; nanny redtail; red stare, with stare meaning starling and red tail. The Redstart was the subject of one of the most remarkable observations of an individual species. John Buxton was captured by the Germans in Norway in 1940 and made a prisoner of war. From his prison he set up observations of breeding Redstart, which was eventually published as a monograph. Aristotle identified the Redstart. As he did not see them in winter he believed in transmogrification, the idea that some species magically change into others i.e. Redstarts became Robins in winter.

The **Redwing** has been migrating to our shores from Scandinavia for centuries hence the bird has acquired a number of local names. These include little feltyfare; red thrush and redwing throlly, from the distinctive red patch on its wing; swine pipe; whin thrush and whindle, both from its whining sound and wind throstle, from the winds that aids the bird's migratory flight.

The **Reed Bunting** is a resident bird found at the margins of reed beds and water. Several local names incorporate sparrow, like pit sparrow; reed sparrow; riverside sparrow and water sparrow, although the two species are not related. Other names refer to the male's distinctive black head, like black bonnet; coaly hood; colin blackhead, again incorporating a human name and seave cap, with seave meaning reed. Unusually the Reed Bunting's song changes after mating with its song becoming more drawn out.

The **Ring Ouzel** is a summer migrant and very much a bird of windswept upland and moors. Its local names refer to this, such as fell blackbird (its close cousin); heath throstle (correctly identified as a member of the Thrush family (Turdidae)); hill ouzel; rock ouzel and tor ouzel. Other names signify its song and call, such as hill chack and ring whistle, from its alarm call. Michaelmas blackbird refers to the time of its migration and round berry bird from the bird's liking of rowan berries.

The **Ringed Plover** breeds on pebble beaches and migrants are often seen on marshes and mud flats. Dullwilly refers to its call; grundling, a Lancashire name, from its habit of running for cover; ring dotterel, with the Dotterel being a similar looking bird; sand laverock, with laverock linking the bird to a lark and suggests betrayal from the bird's habit of feigning injury at the nest when predators appear; sandy lo, with lo being the Nordic for plover; stone hatch from its pebble nest and stone runner, alluding to its environment.

Qi Possibly the most iconic bird in Britain is the **Robin**. In Britain, but not on the continent, the bird associates closely with humans and can become quite tame, especially when food is involved! Ruddock was a reference to the Robin made around 1000 AD, with ruddy as the colour and a suffix of -ock. Redbreast was used as its preferred name until the 20th century. Although the breast colour is more orange, the word orange did not enter the English language until the 16th century, well after the Robin was called red! Another name referring to its colour is robin red-dock. Given its close association with humans many local names incorporated men's names, such as bobby; bob robin; thomas robin and tommy liden. The first postmen, who had vermillion waistcoats, were called Robins, hence the appearance of Robins on Christmas cards, sometimes with a letter in their beak. For a long time the Robin was thought to be the male bird and its female mate was the Wren. In Shetland the Wren was called Robin, where the Robin is rare.

A summer migrant that makes itself heard in reed beds is the **Sedge Warbler**. Until the 18th century there was no distinction between this bird and the very similar Reed Warbler, so some local names refer to both birds. These names include chan chider; chitter chat; irish nightingale; night singer and thorn warbler, all referring to the bird's loud and persistent song. Other names include leg bird, possibly arising from observers being able to see the bird's legs as it straddles reeds whilst singing; fantail warbler, with another species now allocated this as its formal name; the orphean warbler, confusing this bird with the similar continental bird; reed fauvette, with the latter word being French for another warbler; sedge marine; sedge reedling; water sparrow, from the streaky, brown back and willow lark.

The **Scaup** is a sea duck most often observed in winter bobbing up and down on the open sea. The bird's local names reflect its environment, though some names relate it to other ducks, for example black-headed wigeon, frosty-backed wigeon; silver pochard and spoonbill duck. These are in addition to blue neb with neb an old word for bill; covie; dun bird; golden-eyed diver; green-headed diver; holland duck and norway duck. Mussel duck refers to its food and links to the duck's formal English name Scaup, with skalp meaning mussel bed.

Qi The **Shelduck** is a bird of mud flats and marshes and being so large and colourful is easy to pick out. Several local names use the word Goose incorrectly, for example, bar gander referring to the gander's red protuberance on its bill in the breeding season ; links goose; skeeling goose in Orkney and sly goose. Burrow duck comes from the habit of the bird using rabbit burrows for a nest site. At one time the Shelduck was persecuted for disturbing rabbits, when rabbits were an economic source of food. Furze duck refers to the duck's use of gorse at the entrance to the nest. Oddly some females without a nest lay their eggs in another female's nest to make a brood size of up to 30, all of which might hatch! The Shelduck has an unusual moult cycle, moulting all its feathers at once, rather than sequentially like most other birds do. The males, who have little active life with their off-spring, fly off to a gathering place (traditionally the Heligoland Bight in Germany) to moult.

Qi The **Short-eared Owl** is not a common bird but is best seen at twilight hunting low over fields in winter. Our own small population is supplemented during winter by migrants from Scandinavia. Our forebears noticed the arrival of this bird in early winter and gave it names like pilot owl; sea owl and woodcock owl. The first name is based on the story that the bird can be seen flying in from the North Sea at about the same time as the migrating Woodcocks and other birds, and the Owl was said to pilot them in to the safety of our shores. Other names include brown yogle; cat ool; cataface; grey hullet; march owl; moss owl and mouse owl.

The **Shoveler** is a duck with a distinctive bill that is an effective filter of its zooplankton food. The bill contains 200 lamellae which catch the food. Not unsurprisingly many local names refer to this, such as broad bill; scooperbill; shovel bill and spoon-billed teal. Other names include blue-winged stint, with an unclear link, as stint means small; butter duck; mud duck and swaddle duck.

Qi The **Skylark** is a well-known bird of open fields, especially for its non-stop singing from high in the sky when it is heard more often than it seen. Male Skylarks recognise the local variations of their neighbours' song and can identify intruders who do not sing with the local dialect. The local name laverock derives from the Old English lawerce, meaning treason worker. This is based on the bird's habit of landing, from its song flight, a distance away from its well hidden nest to deceive possible predators. The Skylark also uses an injury feigning tactic to draw potential predators away from the nest, putting itself at potential risk, until it startles the predator by flying away! If the song attracts predators when a bird of prey approaches the bird sings louder to deter them. Other local names include lerruck, a derivation of larrock; lintwhite, a name also given to the linnet; melhuez, a Cornish name referring to the Skylark's high flight; rising lark; short-heeled lark and sky flapper. The famous cook, Mrs. Beeton, had a recipe for Skylark, stuffed with bacon, beef and shallots. Skylark numbers have fallen over the last 40 years (to 2012) by 61%, mainly due to changes in farming practice with arable crops being harvested earlier before the young have fledged.

Qi The **Snipe** is a bird that is most often seen as it makes its rapid, zig-zag escape flight when disturbed. The modern word sniper derives from this behaviour as gunmen found the Snipe so hard to shoot because of its escape flight pattern. The word was used by 18th century British soldiers in India to describe shooting from a hidden place. Snipe are so well camouflaged in their grassy wetland environment it is difficult to spot, even close-up. The Snipe breeds in Britain, in wet grassland, but native numbers have decreased by 93% over the last 25 years (to 2012). Numbers increase significantly in winter, supplemented by migrants from the colder continent, Iceland and Scandinavia. Many of its local names refer to the distinctive sound that the male makes during it display flight. As the bird tumbles towards the ground, its two outer tail feathers beat together to make a drumming sound. Hence names like heather bleat; horse gowk, with the sound being compared to a neighing horse and gowk meaning cuckoo and mire bleater. The Old English haerferblaete means billy-goat and bleater similar to gaverhal, from the Celtic meaning goat of the marsh. This distinctive sound is reflected in two poems , the first by John Clare in 'To the snipe' - 'For here thy bill, suited by wisdom good, of rude unseemly length doth delve and drill The gelid mass for food.' and the second by Seamus Heaney in the 'The backward look' - 'A snipe's bleating is fleeing its nesting ground, into dialects, into variants, transliterations whirr on the nature reserves - little goat of the air, of the evening, little goat of the frost, It is his tail feathers drumming elegies in the slipstream.'

The local name full snipe contrasts this bird with its cousin the smaller Jack Snipe. The Snipe's bill is proportionately longer than any other European bird. The bird was shot in large numbers for the table and was relatively cheap, costing 4 pence in the 17th century.

Qi The **Song Thrush** is a well-known bird and is often seen in gardens and the countryside, with its loud and complex song being clearly heard in most seasons, except during summer. However, Song Thrush numbers have decreased by 58% over the last 40 years (Breeding Bird Survey in 2012). Its traditional name is throstle, with thrush the name given to the similar, close relative, the Mistle Thrush. Throstle derives from the Middle English throstel and the Old English prostle, linked to the German drostel. The first written record of the English name Thrush dates from the 8th century. Other names include grey bird; mavis, derived from the French mauvis; thrasher; throggie and whistling dick, referring to its strong song which contains as many as 100 phrases with each phrase repeated twice or three times. Browning captured this in "That's the wise thrush; he sings his song twice over, lest you should think he could never recapture the first fine careless rapture". Thomas Hardy also wrote about the bird in 'The darkling Thrush' - "I leant upon the coppice gate, When frost was spectre grey, And winter's dregs made desolate, The weakening eye of the day... At once a voice arose among, the blackened twigs overhead, In a full-hearted evensong, of joy illimited". Indeed, it is not unusual to hear the bird sing in winter. The Thrush also appears in 'The death and burial of cock Robin' as a singer, 'Who'll sing the psalm', 'I' said the thrush, As she sat in the bush, 'And I'll sing the psalm'.

The use of the word **Sparrow** (or its predecessors) goes back to before the 7th century and has been used as a surname for many centuries. The name was given to a homely or chirpy person.

Qi **Sparrowhawk**s were quite common until numbers fell dramatically in the 1950's. After careful research, it was discovered

that when the bird digested its prey, it also digested the pesticide poison DDT from the prey. This led to very thin egg shells and a subsequent failure to breed. Sparrowhawk numbers did not recover until the 1980's but now is widespread. It is difficult to see the bird as it sits out of sight, ready to pounce on its unsuspecting victims, like the birds on your bird table! Its local names include pigeon hawk, but only the female would stand a chance of catching a pigeon, as she weighs around 260 g, 50% more than the male. Because of its smaller size the male is called a tiercel, from the French la tierce, meaning a third (in size). Other names include blue hawk, for the male which is blue grey on the head and back and blue merlin; hedge hawk, where it sits spying on prey; horse gowk, with the sound being compared to a neighing horse and gowk meaning Cuckoo (having a similar flight silhouette); gold tip, from the colour of the fringes of the feathers and stone falcon. The use of gowk for this bird derives from the traditional tale that the

Cuckoo turned into a Sparrowhawk in winter (before migration was understood). In fact this tale goes back to the time of Homer (thought to be around 800 BC) who reported that the Cuckoo disappeared in winter and turned into a Hierax (probably a Sparrowhawk). Arisotle later disagreed with this, noticing clear differences in plumage between the two birds. The Sparrowhawk is low down in the falconry hierarchy; the female being flown by priests and the male by clerks. Gilbert White in 'The natural history of Selbourne' commented that the Sparrowhawk "was a terror to all the dames in the village that had ducks or chickens under their care". The first written record of the English name for the Sparrowhawk dates from the 8th century.

The **Spotted Flycatcher** was once a common bird being seen sitting on the end of a branch and characteristically flying out to catch an airborne fly and returning to the same perch. Numbers have dropped by 89% over the last 42 years (to2012). Its local names include bee bird; beam bird; cherry chopper, but the bird does not eat cherries; cobweb; post bird from its habit of sitting on a post or branch; spider catcher; wall bird from where it nests; wall robin and white baker.

The **Starling** is a common bird in both urban and rural areas and was familiar to our ancestors. However, numbers have decreased by 81% over the last 40 years (Breeding Bird Survey in 2012) but has recovered to the number two spot in the Garden Birdwatch Survey (2015). One set of local names refers to the habit of Starlings picking off the ticks on a sheep's back, hence the names sheep rack; sheep stare; shepstarling and shepster. Gyp refers to its black colour and stare is an Old English name from the German staro and Old Norse stari, linked to Starling. Pet names include jacob and jebbie. The name stinker derives from the bird's former habit of nesting in the stink pipe of toilets.

The **Stock Dove** has many local names including blue pouter from the way the bird can pout by inflating its crop; burrow pigeon from its habit of nesting in rabbit burrows; craig doo; hill pigeon; hole dove and wood culver associating the bird with woods rather than as a domestic bird.

A bird often heard and seen on gorse covered heaths is the **Stonechat**. Its song is exactly as the names states, like two stones clinked together.

The poet Norman McCaig put it eloquently as "A flint-on-flint ticking - there he is; trim and dandy - in square miles of bracken". Unsurprisingly, many local names refer to its song, such as bushchat; furze chuck; stanechatter; stone clink and stonesmith. Jack straw refers to the Stonechat's use of straw for its nest and jack referring to a small bird and from the man's name. Heath tit is correct for the place it is seen but the bird is in the Thrush and Chat family, Turdidae, not the Tit family, Paridae. However, tit was traditionally used for any small animal. Stonechat numbers have increased by 168% since 1995 (in 2010).

The **Storm Petrel** is a bird of the open oceans and survives atrocious weather conditions, quite remarkable for a small bird weighing 27 g and having a wing span of 38 cm. The Storm Petrel is Britain's smallest sea bird. The bird is a long distance migrant and British birds migrate all the way to southern Africa. Fishermen knew the bird well and gave it many names, including the link to bad weather, hence Storm in the formal name. Witch was a seaman's term for the bird 'hated by sailors, who called them witches, imagining they forbade a storm' along with storm finch. Other local names allude to the bird's habit of ejecting a foul liquid when threatened, like martin oil and oily mootie, with mootie meaning a small thing. The name gorlir refers to the blubber that was taken from the fat fledglings.

Qi A bird closely associated with human habitation is the **Swallow**. Local names are simple ones like barn swallow, which is the bird's international name; chimney swallow; house swallow and red-fronted swallow. The bird almost exclusively nests in buildings and will opportunistically build a nest in new buildings. Swallows are faithful to their nest sites and will return to exactly the same spot as the previous year after their migratory flight from South Africa, and without the use of sat-nav or GPS! In one recent study, 97% of returning males returned to their original nest site. Swallows are breeding earlier as a result of climate warming, typically 3 days earlier each decade since the studies began in 1973. Their insect prey is emerging 4 days per decade earlier, leading to a mis-match between peak insect numbers and the hatching of Swallow chicks. In the 1750's an experiment (conducted by tying coloured threads to their legs) established that birds returned to the same place each year. Females and returning juveniles fly back to the same area. Gilbert White used the name chimney swallow and noted that "it loves to haunt those stacks where there is a constant fire, no doubt for the sake of warmth". The Swallow is the national bird of Estonia and Austria. Elizabeth Barrett Browning wrote 'Anacreon's ode to the swallow' writing 'Thou indeed, little swallow A sweet yearly comer, Art building a hollow New nest every summer, And straight doth depart Where no gazing can follow, Past Memphis, down Nile!' Abraham Cowley wrote in 'The swallow' Foolish prater, what dost thou So early at my window do With thy tuneless serenade? Well't had been had Tereus made Thee as dumb as Philomel.' which refers to the greek myth recounted later in the Section 'Some mythological tales'.

Qi A bird that is sometimes incorrectly thought to be a relative of the Swallow is the **Swift**. Whilst they are both summer visiting, insect eating birds of the air, they come from quite different families and orders. The Swift is in the order Apodiformes and the Swallow in the order Passeriformes. However, a number of local names relate the Swift to the Swallow, such as brown swallow; crane swallow; hawk swallow and tile swallow. Black martin links the bird to the House Martin, which is a close relative of the Swallow. The association of the bird with the devil comes from its screech, which is often heard as small flocks fly around our towns. Hence names like black screech; devil's bitch; devil's squeaker; devil swallow; devil's screecher; horse martin from its horse-like squealing cry; screech martin and shriek owl. Martlet is word used in heraldry as a swallow-like bird with no feet, the word deriving from the French merlette, the name for a small, black bird i.e. merle plus the suffix –ette for small. In fact the Swift has very small and weak feet. It rarely uses them, spending most of its life on the wing. Anchor bird is a Sussex name alluding to its silhouette. The oldest living Swift recorded was 17 years 11 months old. Given that the bird is in constant flight plus and undertakes long migratory journeys, the total distance the bird flew must have been enormous. One estimate is 3 million miles!

The **Tawny Owl** is well known particularly in tales and folk lore. It is more often heard than seen as the Owl is well adapted to a nocturnal life (for details see later). Many of its local names are based on versions of Owl, like howlet, owlet and ullet, all echoic of its famous night time hooting. Names include brown owl; grey owl; hollering owl; screech owl; wood owl plus names including a person's name such as billy hooter; gilly hooter and jenny hoolet. The names beech owl and wood owl derive from where it lives and ivy owl from where it sometimes nests.

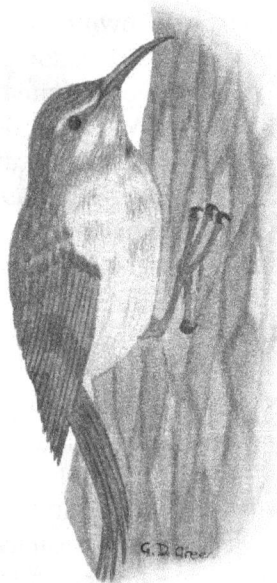

Qi A woodland bird that is usually seen scurrying up the side of a tree, pecking quickly as it goes, is the **Treecreeper**. This habit is reflected in many of its local names like bark creeper; bark runner; common creeper; ox-eye creeper, where the term ox-eye was traditionally used for the tit family, deriving from the French term for a small bird; tree climber, noting that the Treecreeper only ever climbs up a tree (unlike the Nuthatch which can climb down a tree as well) and tree mouse, where mouse is a generic word for the tit family (but this is an incorrect family connection). Cuddy is based on the bird's habit of clinging to the side of a tree, using its tail feathers, which are stiff, to support the bird as it seeks insect food hidden in the bark.

A bird of the seashore that does what its name suggests is the **Turnstone**. However, the bird seems to have been mis-identified, with many local names wrongly linking the bird to other families and species, like horsefoot snipe; red-legged plover; sea dotterel; sea lark; sea quail and skirl crake. Being linked incorrectly to six other species must be a record! With some it is difficult to see the connection! However, ebb picker; stanepicker; stone raw and tangle picker all relate to the Turnstone's feeding habits as it moves along the shore line turning over stones and seaweed to disturb its food.

The black and white coloration of the **Tufted Duck** gives rise to a range of interesting local names, like black curre; black poker; black topping duck; black wigeon; golden-eye duck; magpie duck and white-sided duck. As a diving duck (as opposed to a dabbling duck) it prefers deeper water; the bird can dive to a depth of 2m.

The **Water Rail** is far more numerous than sightings indicate. The bird skulks in reed beds and only exits for a short time or when the weather is severe. It is heard more often than seen. Local names refer to the bird's habit of running from cover to cover, like bilcock with bult meaning to move quickly; darcock; jack runner; rat hen; skitty cock with skite meaning to run quickly and velver runner. Other names include brook ouzel, with a strange reference to a Thrush; gutter cock and weir cock. The word rail was also used to refer to the Corncrake, when the tale was that the Corncrake (a summer migrant) turned into a Water Rail in winter. The expression 'thin as a rail' is associated with this bird's slender body.

Qi A bird often seen near the coast migrating on its way to and from open moorland is the **Wheatear**. Many of its local names are based on some detailed observations of its behaviour, such as clot bird, from its habit of moving from clod to clod; coney chuck from its habit of nesting in rabbit burrows; Cornish horse smatch with the bird attracted to flies on horse dung; fallow chat from the land it inhabits and stone clack as it moves from stone to stone. White arse comes from its prominent white rump (arse not previously being vulgar) along with white rump and white tail and ear bird from its ear stripe. The bird was caught in large numbers for the table, using a noose. A record from Beachy Head (still a good place to see this bird on migration) is of a shepherd catching 1200 birds!

A summer migrant that sings from our hedgerows in summer is the **Whitethroat**. Many local names refer to its nesting material with names like cut straw; hay tit, with tit being a small creature; jack straw using a man's name; nettle creeper, from its habit of nesting in nettles; small straw, from the fine pieces of hay used in its nest; straw mouse (again using mouse for a small creature) and windle straw from Shropshire, where windle means a stalk of withered grass. The bird has names linked to female first names such as great peggy and jennie. Muffie refers to the distinctive white throat, seen well when it sings. Its song is reflected in the name wheetie. White lintie links this bird with the Linnet (lintie) but the Whitethroat is in Warbler family (Sylviidae) not in the Finch family (Fringiliidae). Hedge chicken; feather bird and meg cut-throat are all interesting names but of unclear meaning! In the 1960's the numbers of Whitethroat fell dramatically due to drought in its winter quarters in the Sahel, south of the Sahara desert but numbers have recovered into the 21st century.

The **Whimbrel** looks very similar to the Curlew so many local names make this link. Being slightly smaller, predictably names include foolish curlew; half curlew; jack curlew (again jack denoting small); little whaup and summer whaup, with whaup meaning curlew, but the bird is only seen in summer in northern Scotland, where it breeds. Seven whistler refers to its whistling call. Other names are crooked-bill marlin; striped head and tang whaup, which means seaweed curlew.

The **Wigeon** over-winters on Britain's estuaries and lakes in large numbers. The name half duck refers to its size leading in times past to a lower value at market. Whew and whistler refer to the duck's clear whistle that is redolent of winter bird watching on marshes and estuaries. Other names include easterling; golden head and lady fowl, the first two names are for young birds sold at market.

The **Willow Warbler** is still a common summer visitor and has been for centuries. Visually it is very similar to its close relative the Chiffchaff, so some names also confuse the two birds. However, both birds have very different and distinctive songs. Being a familiar bird some local names include human names, such as fell peggy; ground issac; sally picker; sweet billy and willie muftie. This family of warblers were given the general name wren, although they are not related to the Wren, with names such as golden wren; ground wren; muffie wren and willow wren. Other names like bank jug; feather poke (but the bird does not use feathers in its nest) and ground oven refer to their distinctive nest, which, like the Long-tailed Tit, is domed. Further names include huck muck; nettle bird; smooth and willow sparrow.

The **Woodpigeon** is still a common bird and not much loved by farmers, as it has a voracious appetite for seeds. Local names include clatter dove, referring to the noise of their wings as they take off and Dove is inter-changeable with Pigeon; cow prise; cushat, deriving from cuscote, alluding to the bird's rapid flight; cushy-do; dow; queese, from its voice associated with the Latin questus meaning lament; ring dove from the white feathers on its neck; timmer doo (with doo meaning dove) and wood culver, a 12th century name for a woodland bird. The young birds are called squabs, which is a culinary term for the meat of young birds.

Qi One of our best known birds is the **Wren**. As a mark of this the Wren appeared on the farthing coin from 1937 until the coin was

withdrawn in 1960. It readily associates with human habitation and the Wren has been given a variety of names over the centuries. Some of its local names include human first names such as the well-known jenny wren plus bobby wren; giller wren (from Gill); kitty wren (from Katherine) and sally. Cutty and scut as names refer to the Wren's short tail. There are a range of regional variations based on the bird's diminutive size with puggy wren from Surrey; stumpy toddy from

Cheshire; tiddy wren from Essex; titty todger from Devon and wrannock from Scotland, where –ock is a diminutive suffix.

One of our strangest birds is the **Wryneck**. Technically it is a member of the Woodpecker family, Picidae, but that is not obvious when you see the bird. Like Woodpeckers they have a long tongue used to extract insects from the ground or bark, hence the names long tongue and snake bird. In fact the Wryneck has the longest tongue of all birds, relative to its size. The name rind bird comes from the way the bird feeds on insects found in bark. Rinding means to strip bark, which is carried out at the time the migrant bird arrives. Pee bird (Surrey) and peel bird (Sussex) are from the pee pee sound it makes and snake bird is from the hissing sound the bird makes when threatened. Strangely many of the Wryneck's local names are associated with the Cuckoo. Keen observers noted that the bird arrived just before the Cuckoo, hence the names cuckoo's leader; cuckoo's marrow, from the Midlands where marrow means mate; cuckoo's mate; cuckoo's messenger and cuckoo's waker. Emmet hunter refers to the bird's diet of ants.

The **Yellow Wagtail** is a summer visitor and was well known to our forebears. The bird is often found following cattle and sheep to pick up the flies that are attracted to the animals' dung, hence the name cow bird. Other names include barley bird from the time of arrival of the bird; quaketail; sunshine bird; wagstart and yellow molly. The names moll washer; peggy washer and washerwoman all refer to the up and down movement of the tail, simulating the use of the battledore, a device for beating washing.

Finally, a popular bird of open farmland and hedgerows is the **Yellowhammer**. Inevitably one of its local names is little-bit-of-bread-and-no-cheese, being a representation of its song, which can often be heard clearly as the bird perches at the top of a bush or hedge to make itself heard. Many local names refer to the bright yellow colouration of the male with names like golden amber; gouldie; yellow an-bird; yellow bunting, which was the preferred formal name until the 19th century; yellow homber and yellow yoit. Bessy blakeling combines a female name and a local name for yellow and the suffix –ling. The bird's eggs have exquisite fine line markings on them and local names include scribbling lark, (except the bird is a Bunting not a Lark); writing lark and writing master. The serpent like marks on the eggs have led to the Welsh name servant-of-the-snake, from the myth that the markings warned snakes of predators. Two other local names that seem contradictory are pretty-pretty creature and may-the-devil-take-you, the latter an alternative imitative local name!

FORMAL ENGLISH NAMES

The previous section illustrated the many and varied local names given to birds over the centuries. Many are now obsolete, some have survived. However, to use a range of names for single species, some of which are mis-leading, gives rise to confusion with identification. Attempts were made, from the 17th century onwards to provide a definitive list of British bird names that everyone would agree to use. This endeavour was not complete until the 20th century not least because securing agreement was very difficult. In addition ornithologists still needed to achieve clarity on the identification of some species in order to provide an accurate name. A few official names are still inaccurate but we have to live with them now.

The definitive list is now compiled and published by the British Ornithologists' Union. In fact there are two sets of English names published along with the internationally agreed scientific name.

The first set is the vernacular English name. This is the definitive English name to be used in Britain e.g. in publications, scientific papers and guide books. Some have changed over the years. For example, the 1923 list still called a Tit, Titmouse and the Robin, Robin Redbreast. The written convention is that with vernacular English names each word is capitalised, unless hyphenated, when the second word is lower case e.g. Black-backed Gull.

The second set of English names is the internationally agreed name to be used worldwide but mainly outside Britain. Many names are the same but some are different. For example, Bittern becomes Eurasian Bittern and Chaffinch becomes Common Chaffinch. This is to remove any confusion where similarly named birds of different species occur in other countries, with the agreed names needing to accurately differentiate between them.

The derivation of some bird names are obvious and need no explanation. The Blackcap has a black cap! The Dipper dips! Others are far less obvious and some have an interesting history.

Below is a selection of vernacular English bird names and their derivation. This section commences with an explanation of the names of birds sharing a family name e.g. Tit or Gull, rather than repeat the information for each species. After that a look at birds named by a characteristic e.g. colour. A short section on mis-named birds is followed by an alphabetical list of the derivation and meaning for many individual birds.

Family names

First, some examples of names given to groupings of birds. Most of the groupings are families, to use the taxonomic word.

The Bunting family (Emberizidae) includes the **Corn Bunting**, once a

Corn Bunting

much more common bird than now, the **Cirl Bunting**, once a widespread species but now confined to areas of Devon, with cirl from the Italian to chirp and the **Reed Bunting**. The **Yellowhammer** is also a member of this family. Bunting means a plump or thickset person and appears in the lullaby "baby, baby bunting, father's gone a-hunting". The verb to bunt means to belly out in the wind like a sail. The **Snow Bunting** is now no longer classified as a member of the Bunting family of Emberizidae but is placed in the Calcariidae family. This is an example of how the latest research can lead to the re-classification of a bird.

Divers (the family Gaviidae) are a group with an ancient ancestry and are primitive birds. The group includes the Great Northern Diver, the Red-throated Diver and the Black-throated Diver.

The **Goose families** (the families Anserinae and Branta) consists of several winter migrants who fly considerable distances to escape the winter in their northerly breeding places, such as Siberia, Svalbard, Iceland, Greenland and the Faroes. The group includes the **Barnacle Goose, Bean Goose, Brent Goose, Canada Goose, Greylag Goose, Pink-footed Goose** and the **White-fronted Goose**. The Canada Goose was introduced to Britain in the 17th century as a parkland bird and it was not until the 19th century that it became established in the wild. Technically goose refers to the female, gander to the male and gosling to the young before fledging. Geese are commonly described as silly, as in the proverb that "it is a silly goose that comes to the fox's sermon". A silly person is sometimes called a goose. In a remarkable insight into bird migration the Bishop of Skalholt from Iceland said of these birds in the 17th century 'I speak of fowl which come from abroad; t'out the winter they do not dwell amongst us... every autumn they make for neighbouring countries of England and Scotland...'.

The Finch family name (Fringillidae) derives from the Old English word fink that means a colourful, singing bird. The word entered the language as a surname, from a nickname for someone who handled or bred the birds. Birds in the Finch family with Finch in their name, include **Bullfinch, Chaffinch, Goldfinch, Greenfinch** and **Hawfinch**. Others in this family include **Brambling, Crossbill, Linnet, Redpoll, Serin, Siskin** and **Twite**. Finches were popular as cage birds for both their colour and their song, and were kept in captivity well into the 19th century until campaigning groups changed the practice. Strangely the normally quiet **Bullfinch** was kept as a caged bird because it can be taught to sing. The Bullfinch was such a good singing cage bird that they were traded. Hardy, in Tess of the D'Urbervilles wrote that one of Tess' chores was to whistle to the caged Bullfinch, presumably to teach it a song. In Germany there were Bullfinch academies! The birds were kept in a darkened room and music was played to them. As they copied a few notes (which they do very well) a little light was let in and this process continued, for about 9 months, until the birds could sing the whole song unaccompanied. Experiments have shown that the bird imprints onto humans (in the same way Geese did in the famous Lorenz's experiments) and it is thought that they learn to sing to please their human adoptive parents.

The word **Godwit**, used for the **Black-tailed** and **Bar-tailed Godwit**, derives from the Old English words god for good and wit for creature. Good refers to how good they were to eat, being a feature of medieval banquets.

The **Grebe** family (in the order Podicipediformes) include the **Black-necked Grebe**, the **Great Crested Grebe**, **Little Grebe**, **Red-necked Grebe** and **Slavonian Grebe**. As a group these birds are rarely seen on land and are the most aquatic family of birds in the world as they live wholly on water including nesting on water.

Gull, which appears in several birds' names, comes from the word for someone that will swallow anything thrown at them. How true! The word also means to trick or deceive. The Herring Gull will eat any fish, not just herring. It has learned to drop mussels on a hard surface to break the shell. Young Herring Gulls will abandon their parents and attach themselves to another pair if they think they will be better fed! Fledglings are stimulated to feed by the red band on their parents' bill. In fact they be can be fooled into begging for food from an artificial bill with a red band on it, behaviour known as super normal stimuli. The young birds feed until their weight exceeds that of their parents. The first written record of the English name for the **Herring Gull** dates from the 8th century. Gulls are in the family Laridae. Other British birds with Gull in their name are **Audouin's Gull, Black-headed Gull, Bonaparte's Gull, Caspian Gull, Common Gull, Glaucous Gull, Great Black-backed Gull, Iceland Gull, Lesser Black-backed Gull, Little Gull, Mediterranean Gull** and **Yellow-legged Gull**.

Harriers (of which there are three in Britain – the Hen, Marsh and Montagu's) are named from their behaviour of pursuing and destroying their prey, hence the verb to harry. The **Hen Harrier** derives its names from its habit of chasing hens, the **Marsh Harrier** from its habitat and **Montagu's** from the person who correctly identified this species separating it from the similar Hen Harrier. The Harriers presented early ornithologists with quite an identification challenge. It was thought that the male **Hen Harrier** and the male (of what we now call) **Montagu's Harrier** were a pair, called a Hen Harrier and the respective females were a pair, called ringtails. This confusion arose because the male and female birds of both species have a very different appearance and the females are larger. The true identification was made by George Montagu in the late 18th century.

The name for the **Lark family** comes from a Germanic name for a little songster. Larks are renowned songsters, such as the **Shore Lark**, **Skylark** and **Woodlark**, giving rise to the phrase 'to sing like a lark'.

Larks were kept as cage birds and were subject to the extreme cruelty of being blinded to allegedly make them sing better. Larks are in the family Alaudidae.

Owls are well known throughout history and have interacted with people in Britain for centuries, hence there are plenty of local names and many tales and myths surrounding this group. These Owls include the **Barn Owl, Little Owl, Long-eared Owl, Short-eared Owl, Snowy Owl** and **Tawny Owl**. Owls are in the family Strigidae, except the Barn Owl which is in the Tytonidae family. The word Owl derives onomatopoeically from the bird's howl, coming from the Anglo Saxon ule and Latin ulula to howl. Ululate means to wail or lament loudly, deriving from the Roman for Owl.

The name **Petrel**, in the family of birds Hydrobatidae, comes from their habit of pattering their feet on waves as they fly very close to the surface of the sea. This is linked to St Peter, who attempted to walk on the sea. Unusually for birds this family have a good sense of smell, helping them to locate food whilst at sea. Birds include **Leach's Petrel, Storm Petrel** and **Wilson's Petrel**.

The **Pipit** family Motacillidae, includes the **Meadow Pipit, Richard's Pipit, Rock Pipit, Tawny Pipit, Tree Pipit** and **Water Pipit**. Pipit derives from the Latin 'pipeo' meaning chirper.

Birds in the **Plover** family (Charadriidae) whose names incorporate the word plover include **Golden Plover, Grey Plover, Kentish Plover,**

Little Ringed Plover

Little Ringed Plover and **Ringed Plover**. Plover derives from two possible sources. One is the Norman plovier, linked to the bird's clear call and the word French plovere and the Latin pluvia, meaning rain, though the connection of rain specifically to the Plover family is unclear. The **Dotterel** and **Lapwing** also belong to this family.

The large **Sandpiper** family (Scolopacidae) comprises birds with names like **Common Sandpiper, Curlew Sandpiper, Green Sandpiper, Marsh Sandpiper, Pectoral Sandpiper, Purple Sandpiper, Semi-palmated Sandpiper** and **Wood Sandpiper**. The -piper in Sandpiper is simply onomatopoeic.

Shearwaters (Procellariidae) get their name from the way in which their wing tips just cut through the tops of waves as they fly on stiff wings at right angles to the sea. Birds in this family include the **Balearic Shearwater, Cory's Shearwater, Great Shearwater, Manx Shearwater** and **Sooty Shearwater**.

The **Shrike** family (Laniidae) include the **Great Grey Shrike, the Lesser Grey Shrike, Red Backed Shrike** and the **Woodchat Shrike**. Shrike derives from the Old English word scric, echoic of its loud, shrieking cry.

The **Skua** family (Stercorariidae) includes **Arctic Skua, Great Skua** and **Pomarine Skua** with Skua deriving from the Norwegian skuvur and the Old Norwegian skufr which derives from the bird's call.

Swans (Anserinae) include **Bewick's Swan, Mute Swan** and **Whooper Swan**. Swan derives from the Old English swan, akin to the German schwan and Dutch zwaan which in turn derived from Indo-European root swen (to sound, to sing), whence the Latin sonus (sound).

The **Tern** family (Laridae) includes the **Arctic Tern, Black Tern, Common Tern, Little Tern, Roseate Tern** and **Sandwich Tern**. Up until the 18th century Terns were called sea swallows. It is easy to see why when watching them flying over the sea, showing their prominent tail streamers. Tern derives from the Old English stearn which is onomatopoeic. The Arctic Tern enjoys more daylight hours than any other bird, as it migrates from polar north to polar south each year. One Swedish study in 2016 tracked a bird that covered 96 000 km in one year. This is well over the 40 000km circumnavigation journey as it includes all its rest stops and other movements and deviations. This bird holds the record for the furtherest British ringing recovery, with one bird ringed on Anglesey being recovered in Australia 18 000km away.

The **Tit** family (Paridae) name is an abbreviation of titmouse, a word from the 14th century, when tit was used generically for any small

Coal Tit

creature and mouse referred to the Tit family. Names in this family include **Blue Tit, Coal Tit, Crested Tit, Great Tit, Marsh Tit** and **Willow Tit**. As explained later the **Bearded Tit** is not now in this family, being mis-named. Also the Long-tailed Tit is in the separate family of Aegithalidae.

The **Warblers** (Sylviidae) are another large family and birds whose name includes warbler are **Cetti's Warbler, Dartford Warbler, Garden Warbler, Grasshopper Warbler, Marsh Warbler, Reed Warbler, Savi's Warbler, Sedge Warbler, Willow Warbler** and **Wood Warbler**.

Wagtail (Motacillidae) appears in the name of the **Grey Wagtail, Pied Wagtail** and the **Yellow Wagtail**.

The **Woodpecker** family (Picidae) include **Great Spotted Woodpecker, Green Woodpecker, Lesser Spotted Woodpecker** and **Wryneck**.

Characteristics groupings

Many bird's name derive from some key characteristic based on our observations of the bird.

BIRD SONG. One obvious characteristic is basing the bird's name on its song or call. Bird song has been such a part of our lives that many names represent what we hear:

Several birds' names are a phonetic representation of a bird's song i.e. onomatopoeic. For example, **Chiffchaff; Chough; Curlew; Cuckoo**; the **Grasshopper Warbler** sounds like a fisher's reel as it emits 1400 double notes a minute (as many as 250 000 notes a night); **Kittiwake**; **Quail** and **Water Rail** from the French rale, a death rattle connected to this secretive bird's scraping noise. Similarly for groups of birds such as **Chats**; **Larks**, a Germanic name for a songster; **Owls**, from their howl; **Plovers**, from the Old French plouvier related to the bird's clear call and **Warblers**. The **Mute Swan** is generally a very quiet bird, unlike its close relative the **Whooper Swan** which has an accurate onomatopoeic name. **Sandpiper** refers to the birds' shrill call. **Pipit** derives from the Latin pipeo, meaning a chirper. **Twite** is a representation of the bird's tweet call. The **Whimbrel**'s name is based on the bird's whimpering call, becoming whimmer plus the suffix – erel; **Wood Warbler** and **Woodpeckers** have a special means of attracting attention, by drumming usually on wood, to set up a resonance at a specific frequency. It hits timber between 10 and 14 times a second.

APPEARANCE.

Another notable feature of birds is their colour and appearance. A number of birds' names derive from this including **Blackbird; Blackcap; Blue Tit** - the blue cap of the male emits ultra violet light which the female can see (but we can't); **Bullfinch**, from its bulky appearance; **Coal Tit; Common Crossbill; Common Scoter** is from sooter i.e. black as soot; **Firecrest; Goldcrest; Golden Eagle; Goldeneye; Goldfinch; Great Crested Grebe** – historically this bird's head feathers were used in millinery; **Green Sandpiper; Green Woodpecker; Greenfinch; Grey Wagtail; Long-tailed Duck; Pintail; Pink-footed Goose; Razorbill; Shelduck** with sheld meaning varigated; **Short-eared Owl**, where in fact the face tufts are not ears but are decorative; **Tufted Duck; Waxwing; Whitethroat** and **Yellowhammer**.

Common in a bird's name, like **Common Gull** and **Common Scoter** means having no particular distinguishing features, rather than being numerous.

FEEDING HABITS.

Bean Goose from the birds winter feeding habits; **Carrion Crow**; **Chaffinch**, from the historic habit of the bird eating the chaff from threshing grain; **Kingfisher** and **Oystercatcher**, with British birds preferring to eat mussels and clams and not oysters. The name **Sparrowhawk** is not entirely correct as the female is able to take much bigger prey, such as Pigeons. The female weighs about 260 g compared to the smaller male, weighing as little as 150 g. This difference allows the male to take smaller birds, such as Sparrows, to feed the fledglings. This accounts for why the Sparrowhawk breeds slightly later in the season so that other, smaller birds' chicks have already fledged ready for the male Sparrowhawk to catch as food for its younger chicks. It has been estimated that in one year each Sparrowhawk kills 30 kg of prey and eats about 20 kg of this. One study revealed that 82% of prey killed weighed less than 50 g but this only made up 47% of the total weight of prey killed. The balance being made up of heavier birds, up to 350 g weight. The **Turnstone** is aptly names being seen scurrying along the shore line turning over stones to catch its food.

Q_i **EPONYMS.** One of the ultimate accolades for a naturalist or ornithologist is to have an animal or bird named after you i.e. an eponym. In the world of birds several species have been named after famous people, often experts in the subject. On the British list there are 36 birds named after individuals. These include **Audouin's Gull, Bewick's Swan, Cetti's Warbler** and **Savi's Warbler**. Some people are held in high esteem and have several birds named after them, with Pallas taking the prize with four species on the British list named after him – Pallas' Grasshopper Warbler, Reed Bunting, Sandgrouse and Warbler. Pallas was born in Berlin in 1741, travelled throughout Europe, undertook expeditions to Siberia, worked in St Petersburg and wrote many books. He also proposed a classification for birds into 7 orders and 68 families containing 425 birds. Gilbert White, famed for his innovative study of birds (recorded in the book *The Natural History and Antiquities of Selborne*), was commemorated with a (non-British) bird named after him - White's Thrush.

Qi **HUMAN NAMES.** As we saw in the section on local names, some birds utilise human names, as do some formal names. **Guillemot** comes from the French Guillaume (William). **Robin** is derived from a pet name for Robert. **House Martin** and **Sand Martin** from the Norman name of Martin, associated with the god of war, Mars. **Jack Snipe** utilises the human name Jack to denote small, as does the first part of the name **Jackdaw**, with the suffix –daw being a general name for a member of the Crow family. Daw also means knave or someone held in low esteem.

ENVIRONMENT. Several formal birds' names come from the bird's environment. These include the **Corn Crake; House Sparrow; Marsh**

Harrier; Reed Warbler; Sedge Warbler; Water Rail; Woodcock and **Woodlark**.

PLACES. A number of birds are named after places or regions, some are accurate, others not. The **Kentish Plover** formerly breed in Kent but not now and is only seen infrequently as a visitor from the continent. One of Britain's lightest birds (weighing 10 g) is the **Dartford Warbler** which is named after the place where a pair was shot. It was commonplace for ornithologists who wanted a closer look at a bird to have one shot, inspect it close up and perhaps give it to a museum as a specimen. The **Manx Shearwater** is from the Isle of Man (or more accurately the Calf of Man) remaining there only after efforts were made to eradicate rats from the island, which almost eliminated the bird. The **Sandwich Tern** is named after the place in Kent, where specimens of the bird were sent from. Three Gulls are named after regions – **Mediterranean Gull, Iceland Gull** and **Caspian Gull** and two Terns, the **Arctic Tern** and **Caspian Tern**. Others include the **Arctic Skua** and **Scottish Crossbill**.

Mis-named birds

Historically a number of anomalies existed and several have been tidied up. For example, what is now the **Dunnock** was originally called a Hedge-Sparrow (in the 1923 BOU list). However, the bird is a member of the Prunellidae family rather than the Passeridae family of the Sparrows. Also, looking at the thin bill indicates the bird is not a Sparrow! Other anomalies remain:

Bearded Tit is another of the few formal names that is inaccurate. The

bird superficially looks like a Tit but is actually from the Timaliidae family, a different family altogether. It is the only British member of that family and it has no near relatives. Also the bird has a moustache not a beard!

The 'mar' in **Fulmar** is an old word for Gull but the bird is a tubenose, related to the Albatross rather than a Gull. Gulls are in a separate order (Chadriiformes) from the Fulmar (Procellariiformes).

The name **Goosander** derives from the word Goose but the bird is a saw-tooth not a goose, being in the Mergini family!

The **Honey-buzzard**, is completely mis-named! The bird does not eat honey, although it eats bees wasp grubs, having adapted not to be stung by them as it forages through a nest! The bird is closely related to the Kites rather than to Buzzards.

The **Long-tailed Tit** is mis-named as a Tit as it is not in the Tit family Paridae but in the separate family (with no other British bird) of Aegithalidae.

Qi The tuft of feathers on the top of the heads of the **Long-eared Owl** and the **Short-eared Owl** are mis-named. Both have tufts but these are not ears. The tufts might have a function in changing the shape of the ear to enhance the Owl's hearing but they are probably mainly decorative for use in looking fierce! As with other Owls, the birds have an acute sense of hearing. Whilst they have good vision, their hearing is highly sensitive and is used to locate prey accurately. This ability makes the birds highly proficient night hunters. The large ears are located in the birds' facial discs, behind feathers that accentuate the hearing. The ears are placed asymmetrically on each side, giving the bird stereo hearing, as sound arrives at each ear at a slightly different time. The difference is about 30 millionths of a second, but it does the job! The section of the brain which analyses sound is proportionately larger.

Qi The **Stone-curlew** is not a Curlew but is in the Burhinidae family, commonly called thick-knees. The name curlew comes from its call being similar to the Curlew. Even the name thick-knee is incorrect! The thick joint that can be seen on the leg of the bird is in fact the equivalent of the human ankle, not the knee! The knee joint in birds is nearly always hidden underneath feathers. The local names for this poor bird repeatedly associate it with the wrong family, with a range of names like great plover; thick-kneed bustard; night hawk and willie reeve. The BOU recommends that where the family name is incorrect, a hyphen is used to separate the two words i.e. Stone-curlew and the second word is in lower case.

The **Snow Bunting** has been re-located into Calcariidae family from the Bunting family (Emberizidae) as the result of DNA analysis. So its formal English name places it in the wrong family.

Individual bird names

Below are a number of individual bird's names in alphabetical order with their meaning and derivation explained:

The **Avocet** gets its name from its black cap, as once worn by European advocates or lawyers.

Qi The next bird illustrates the way in which a myth can become accepted as true and embedded into the bird's name - the **Barnacle Goose**. In 1185 the Welsh cleric Giraldus reported "They (i.e. the birds) are produced from fir timber tossed along the sea, and are at first like gum. Afterwards they hang down by their beaks as if they were a seaweed attached to the timber, and are surrounded by shells in order to grow more freely. Having thus in process of time been clothed with a strong coat of feathers, they either fall into the water or fly freely away into the air. They derived their food and growth from the sap of the wood or from the sea, by a secret and most wonderful process of alimentation. I have frequently seen, with my own eyes, more than a thousand of these small bodies of birds, hanging down on the sea-shore from one piece of timber, enclosed in their shells, and already formed. They do not breed and lay eggs like other birds, nor do they ever hatch any eggs, nor do they seem to build nests in any corner of the earth." This tale was repeated over the centuries, including by John Gerard in the 16th century, being affirmed as a truth. Bishops in Ireland declared that as the Goose was not 'born of flesh' i.e. not meat, they could be eaten during Lent. At the time observers in Britain did not know that the bird migrated north in summer to breed on the island of Spitzbergen. Latterly barnacle became adopted as the formal name for the bird. The first written record of the English name for the Barnacle Goose dates from the 8th century.

The **Bittern**'s name has a long history and its roots seem to be in the Latin butio, from a bird that roars like an ox whilst mating. Then into the Old French butor and so on to bitore, bittor, bitterne and finally Bittern. Several bird names make a gradual change over time, with a few letters changing each time but eventually morphing to something quite different.

The Bittern was extinct in Britain as a breeding bird between the 1870s and 1911. In the 20th century numbers recovered and then fell to a low of 11 booming males in 1997. Recently (2017) numbers have increased to 164 booming males at 71 sites as a result of conservation efforts. As well as loss of habitat Bitterns were taken by taxidermists and egg collectors. There are thought to be more stuffed Bitterns in Norfolk than there are live birds!

The **Black Redstart** and its close relative the Redstart end in the word start. This was the word for tail, used until the 16th century, coming from the Middle English steort. The first written record of the English name for the Redstart dates from the 8th century. Several local names use the word start like wagstart for the Yellow Wagtail.

Brambling refers to the striking plumage of this winter visiting Scandinavian Finch, possibly from the word brandling meaning branded. Its summer plumage is even more striking than the duller winter plumage we see in Britain. The bird forms very large flocks in winter, with one Swiss flock in 1951 reported as containing an estimated 7 million birds.

The **Brent Goose** is a winter visitor to fields of eel grass, its favourite food. Brent derives from brant and is onomatopoeic for the guttural call of the bird.

The **Buzzard**'s name comes from falconry where the name meant 'useless kind of hawk' although it was flown by a baron in the falconry hierarchy (one level below the Peregrine). In America the word is now used as derogatory expression for someone who is worthless or stupid, but there the name is also used for the Turkey Vulture. Dr Johnson described the bird as 'a degenerate or mean species of hawk' and Bewick as 'cowardly, inactive and slothful'. The Buzzard's eyes are proportionately 50 times the size of a human eye and give about 45° binocular vision and 150° monocular vision. The eyes cannot rotate in their sockets and are protected by a nictating membrane and an eyebrow.

Qi The **Carrion Crow**'s name derives from eating carrion as part of its diet and the second word from its raucous sound. The bird's character has given rise to a number of well known phrases, for example the commonly used 18th century phrase 'as the crow flies' meaning the distance in a straight line between two places. The Crow does not particularly fly in a straight line but the phrase has stuck. Alfred Hitchcock used the birds as a frightening, dark influence in the film The Birds. The Crow is the fourth most widespread bird in Britain. Numbers of the bird have doubled in the last 40 years (to 2010). In Scotland and Ireland the sub-species the Hooded Crow takes the place of the all-black Carrion Crow that resides elsewhere. The first written record of the bird's name in English is from 662 AD.

The **Capercaillie** is a large bird from the Scottish highlands that emits a loud sound to attract females. It is so loud the bird's ears have a reflex stopping action to prevent the bird going deaf from its own song! Capercaillie derives from the Gaelic words capull and coille, literally horse of the woods. The nuptial song is likened to the sound of horses' hoofs on cobbles. The Capercaillie was killed as game and became extinct late in the 18th century. The present population derives from birds introduced in the 19th century. The Capercaillie is the world's largest grouse.

Cetti's Warbler is a bird mostly heard and not often seen, with a distinctive very loud song resembling gun-fire. David Turner in his book 'Was Beethoven a birdwatcher?' suggests that the explosive opening bars of the fourth movement of Beethoven's second symphony were inspired by the bird's song. Up to the 1950's the bird was rarely seen in Britain but numbers have increased by 240% since 1998 (to 2010). It first bred in Britain in 1973 and is expanding its range year by year.

Qi The **Chiffchaff** is one of the first summer migrants to arrive and one of the last to leave. Its name is onomatopoeic and its repetitive song is commonly heard throughout the summer. However, whilst we hear the song as a repetition of two notes one analysis discovered 47 variations, which presumably the females can distinguish in order to choose a mate. Occasionally the Chiffchaff cross breeds with its close relative the Willow Warbler and the off-spring sing part of a Chiffchaff's song and part Willow Warbler's! The bird needs to eat 2.5g of flies each day; a third of its own weight. Before migrating the bird's weight increases from 7.5g to over 9.0g, laying down fat for energy. Wintering birds seen in Britain are continental birds that migrate here.

The cirl of the **Cirl Bunting**'s name derives from the Latin to chirp, with bunting meaning plump or thick-set. The Cirl Bunting was comparatively common across England in the 1930's and gradually its range has diminished until it is now confined to a few areas of Devon.

The **Common Scoter**'s name comes from soot, referring to the bird's dark colour. An alternative source is the Old English sceotan, meaning to move rapidly (leading to the modern word scoot). The bird was declared fish, rather than fowl, and so could be eaten during Lent.

The **Coot**'s formal name is onomatopoeic.

Qi The name **Cormorant** derives from the Old French cormaran which in turn comes from the Latin names corvus marinus, meaning sea-raven. Of course, the Cormorant is not related to the Raven except they are both very black birds! The Cormorant is considered a pest to fish stocks and licences are issued to cull the bird. In Japan the Cormorant is used by fishermen to catch fish. A noose is tied round the neck of the bird in such a way that it can catch a fish but not swallow it.

The Cormorant is often seen sitting with its wings spread out to dry them. The majority of birds keep their feathers water proof by maintaining their oily covering. When other birds preen they use their bill to collect an oil from their cloaca and spread it around their wings and body feathers. The Cormorant is a superb swimmer and dives to considerable depths to catch fish. Its feathers are not fully oiled (the edges are not water-proofed) to improve the bird's efficiency whilst swimming under water. As a result its feathers get wet and have to be dried. Holding their wings out has a further benefit as it increases blood flow to the stomach which aids digestion. Unlike many other birds, the Cormorant does not have a brood patch which is used to regulate the temperature of their eggs. Instead it uses its large webbed feet to do the same.

The **Cuckoo**'s name is clearly onomatopoeic, but only that of the male's song. The female emits a soft bubbling sound. Research (in Hungary) has shown that male Cuckoos recognise the unfamiliar calls of intruders

to their territory, differentiating them from familiar neighbours. The males reacted aggressively towards these intruders whilst tolerating neighbours. The Cuckoo is famed for always laying its eggs in the nests of other birds. The whole breeding cycle of the Cuckoo is remarkable. Each female only ever lays in the nest of a specific host species, as will her female off-spring. The most common hosts are Dunnock, Meadow Pipit, Pied Wagtail, Reed Warbler, Robin and Sedge Warbler. The eggs she lays mimic the host's eggs in colour and her eggs are proportionately small for the size of bird. The female is able to store sperm for many days. She observes a selected nest and at the right moment starts the 24 hour egg production process. The act of laying an egg takes 3-4 seconds, in which time she ejects one of the host's eggs. At this time she also emits a call mimicking a bird of prey which frightens the host bird and distracts them from the Cuckoo's activity. On average a female lays 9 eggs per year. The young chick, on emerging from the egg immediately and instinctively starts to eject the other eggs from the nest, using a specially developed hollow in its back. The Cuckoo chick has a voracious appetite and increases its weight from 4 g at birth to 16 g in 4 days! The chick's begging call imitates the host species' chicks' call to induce the host adults to feed the bird. The natural history of the Cuckoo took a long time to unfold. Edward Jenner presented a paper to the Royal Society in 1788 giving evidence of the cuckoo's egg laying behaviour. His paper was considered so fantastic that the Royal Society suggested " it is best to give you full scope for altering it". W H Auden wrote about the bird in Short ode to the cuckoo - "Compared to the arias by great performers such as the merle, your two-note act is kid-stuff, our most hardened crooks are sincerely shocked by your nesting habits. Science, Aesthetics, Ethics, may huff and puff , but they cannot extinguish your magic: you marvel the commuter as you wondered the savage. Hence in my diary where I enter nothing but social engagements and, lately, the death of friends, I scribble year after year when I first hear you, of a holy moment." Delius also composed a piece on the Cuckoo's arrival and song in "On hearing the first Cuckoo in spring".

Numbers of Cuckoo have declined by 73% over the past 25 years (to 2009). The oldest living Cuckoo recorded was 6 years 11 months old.

Qi The **Dotterel** is in the Plover family (taxonomically the Charadriidae family) and a rare summer visitor which breeds in the Highlands. The birds are easy to approach and catch. This gives them the name dotard and thence to the modern word dotty, meaning a fool. The diminutive suffix –erel is added. In former days, when the bird was more numerous, it was shot for eating. It is Britain's highest altitude breeding species, seldom breeding at less than 3000 ft. Unusually the female is the brighter coloured bird who performs a song display to attract the male. Having mated and laid her eggs, the female leaves the incubation of the first brood to the male. She is then free to mate with another male and have a second brood in quick succession (which she incubates) to maximise productivity in the short summer period.

The **Dunlin** is a common winter visiting wader that can be seen in large flocks on our estuaries. The winter plumage is quite plain in contrast to its brighter summer plumage which includes a large black belly patch. This seasonal contrast led early naturalists to believe there were two distinct species. The name dun means dull brown colour, reflecting the bird's winter plumage. The diminutive suffix –lin produces an accurate name for one of our smallest waders. The Dunlin migrates long distances, with the adults utilising a southerly route via the Baltic whilst the juveniles make their own way south from their Russian birth grounds via Norway. The North American name for this bird is Red-backed Sandpiper placing it in the correct large family of Scolopacidae, with the Sandpipers.

Qi The **Dunnock's** name is derived in the same manner as the Dunlin, above. Dun is for its dull, brown colour and this time the diminutive suffix –ock is added. The 1923 BOU list of English bird names incorrectly named this bird the Hedge-sparrow. The Dunnock is in Prunellidae family of Accentors not the Passeridae Sparrow family. It was not until 1949 that the name Dunnock was officially adopted. The Dunnock is probably Britain's most promiscuous bird, practicing polygyandry i.e. many females mating with many males. They mate, albeit very quickly, as many times as twice an hour for 10 days. This promiscuity necessitates the male having a large cloacal protuberance associated with sperm competition. How mistaken was a Victorian clergy who advocated that his congregation follow the example of the Dunnock "Unobtrusive, quiet and retiring ... the dunnock exhibits a pattern which many of a higher grade might imitate..."!!

Qi The **Eider** has been famous for its down for many centuries. In the 7th century the hermit Saint Cuthbert gave protection to the birds on Farne Island, hence the local name for bird of cuddy's duck. St Cuthbert hand reared the birds and they attached themselves to him as their protector. This is a very early record of imprinting, where young birds form a bond with humans as though they were their parents. The bird's nest is lined with eiderdown made from feathers plucked from the female's breast. These feathers are harvested (after the young have fledged) for pillows and quilts. Duvet is the French for Eider. The female reduces its heart beat whilst brooding to reduce the chance of detection by a predator, which is a particular threat to ground nesting birds. Eider can eat mussels whole, crushing the shells in their stomach and excreting them. The Eider also holds a British record, being the fastest bird in constant level flight, having been timed at 47 mph. The Eider is the commonest sea-duck in the world and the largest in the northern hemisphere. The word Eider comes from the Icelandic aeour, meaning down duck. The first written record of the English name Eider dates from about 650 AD.

The **Fieldfare**'s name derives from the Anglo-Saxon feldefare, meaning traveller through fields.

Qi The **Fulmar** has a particularly smelly habit of firing off the oily contents of its stomach when approached too closely by an intruder. Some predatory birds' feathers can be so fouled by this oil it disables the bird. This did not stop the bird being trapped for its oil, which was used as a fuel. Martin Martin recorded in 1698 "and when the young fulmar is ready to take wing, he being approached, ejects a quantity of pure oyl out at his bill, and will make sure to hit any that attacks him, in the face .... The inhabitants surprise him from behind by taking hold of his bill, which they tie wuth a thread, and upon their return to home they untie it with a dish under to receive the oyl". St Kildan's lived off the birds, each resident consuming an average of 115 Fulmars a year. Fulmar are truly pelagic birds, spending all their life at sea, except when breeding. Unusually amongst birds the so-called tube-noses have a keen sense of smell. Whilst at sea they navigate using their sense of smell and locate food a several kilometres distant. They are able to fly continuously by using the up-draught from waves to soar and glide and fly with tail winds rather than head winds, to save energy. Ful came from Old Norse into Hebridean, meaning foul plus the general word - mar for Gull. The Fulmar is not even closely related to the Gulls but is in a different taxonomic order, the Procellariiformes (which includes the Albatrosses) and is in the Shearwater family, Procellariidae.

The Fulmar is a slow breeder but a long lived bird, with an average life span of 44 years. Young birds reach breeding maturity at about 9 years old, having spent their early life at sea. They only lay one egg and if this fails they do not re-lay.

The **Gadwall**'s name comes from gaddel, which means incessant chatter.

The name **Gannet** derives from the Latin ganta, merely meaning goose, then later gander. The bird is however in the order Pelecaniformes and the family Sulidae and is not related to geese.

Garganey comes from the raucous call of the female with the Latin gargala meaning 'tracheal artery', an echo of the females' monosyllabic note.

The name **Goshawk** comes from goose hawk although even the larger female weighing 1500 g would find it difficult to catch a goose. The male is smaller, weighing 850 g and was originally given the generic male hawk name of tiercel.

The -lag in the **Greylag**'s English name is probably from the lag-lag call made when driving geese or from the fact that they lagged behind other geese when migrating.

Hobby is from the French 'hobereau' to stir, referring the bird's agility when pursuing prey and how flocks of birds (like Swallows and House Martins) fly off when they see a Hobby. Also there is a link to the French verb 'hober' to jump about hence French name 'faucon hoberau'. Hobby was also the diminutive form of Robert, but the Robin took this name.

The **Jackdaw**, a member of the Crow family Corvidae, readily associates

with humans, often nesting in chimney stacks. Jack means small i.e. a small Crow and daw means knave or someone held in low esteem. It has a reputation as a thief through being attracted to shiny objects. Jackdaw numbers have increased by 140% over the last 40 years (in 2012).

The **Jay**'s name is based on the harsh, sharp sound it makes. The name comes from the Old French jai via the Modern French geai to Jay.

The name **Knot** possibly derives from the bird's association with 11th century King Canute, Knot being an alternative name for the king. The story of Canute appears in the Section 'Some common folk lore'. In one experiment a hand-reared bird, which could not fly, continued to show all the signs of migratory behaviour, including putting on weight (from 130 g to 190 g) and moulting, leading to the conclusion that migratory behaviour is innate. The bird's gizzard changes with the seasons. In winter it is thicker when eating harder food and is thinner in summer when it eats softer food.

Qi The **Linnet** is another singing Finch which was popular as a caged singing bird in the 19th century. Lin comes from the Latin for flax or linseed, which the bird eats, plus the diminutive suffix –et. The Linnet (along with its close relation the Twite) is the only bird to feed seeds to its young. Adult seed-eaters usually feed invertebrates to their young. Linnets, as with many other birds, can learn to sing a variety of songs or to repeat words. Birds have an innate ability to sing but have to learn the specifics of their species' song. So Linnets can be made to acquire a different song by removing young birds from its parents, before it has time to learn the Linnet's song from its parents, and exposing it to the alternative songs to be learned.

The **Little Egret**'s name derives from the French aigrette for the bird's long white head plumes. Up to the 1970's the bird was classified as a rarity. It slowly acclimatised to living in Britain and first bred in 1996. In the 18 years to 2013, numbers increased by 2000%. Similarly this applies to the **Cattle Egret**.

The Stint in the **Little Stint**'s name refers to doing a minimum amount of work and can mean sparingly e.g. not stinting with materials. The bird is very similar to the Dunlin and is seen scurrying around whilst feeding.

Qi The **Magpie**, another member of the Crow family Corvidae, is a familiar bird seen around human habitation. In fact its name has a human connection as the Mag part of the name is a shortened version of Madge and Margaret. Pie originally meant a mixture of colours, but now means black and white (as now in Pied Wagtail). Magpies are omnivorous and will take small birds up to the size of a Blackbird. A study into the effect Magpies had on the breeding success rate and population levels of small birds found there was no connection. The Magpie has been shown to be a highly intelligent animal, with a proportionately large brain (as a % of body mass). As with most

Corvids they exhibit highly social behaviour. Corvids are attracted to shiny objects and will take them. Rossini wrote an opera entitled 'The thieving Magpie' in which a Magpie steels a silver spoon and hides it in its nest, only for it to be found just in time to save Ninetta's life.

The derivation of the name **Mallard** is unclear but possibly derives from the Old French malart or mallart for wild drake. Mallard also has the same root as male.

Qi The **Manx Shearwater** once bred in large numbers on the Calf of Man, hence being named after the place. It ceased to breed by the beginning of the 19th century when the island was over-run by rats. Efforts are being made to re-establish a colony on the Calf of Man as 90% of the world population of the Manx Shearwater breed in Britain. This bird has a complex history of names. Willughby was one of the first in England to catalogue and give names to all the then known British birds. He called this bird the Mank Puffin in 1678, which has continued to cause confusion as clearly the bird is a Shearwater (order Procellariiformes) and not a Puffin (order Charadriiformes). The main connections are that both birds are pelagic, they nest in burrows and both were a source of food. In fact the name Puffin derives from an older word pophyn, referring to the cured carcasses of nestling Shearwaters. The oldest living Manx Shearwater recorded was 50 years 11 months old. The Manx Shearwater is a long-haul migrant and flies all the way to the South American coast, a journey of over 6000 miles. The 50 year old bird referred to flew about 600 000 miles on its migratory flights alone and an estimated total of 5 million miles! In an experiment a bird was taken to Venice and released. In 14 days it arrived back at its nest site, demonstrating that birds have a strong migratory instinct. The birds nest in close packed colonies and the fledglings sitting in their nest hole recognise the individual calls of their parents and reply, to assist the parent in finding the nest.

The name **Merlin** may have come from the 15th C merlyon and the Anglo Norman merillon deriving from the Latin merula - Blackbird (now part that bird's scientific name), which is occasionally taken by the Merlin.

Qi The **Mute Swan** is our only resident Swan. The bird is not mute; although it does not have a song it can make a series of sounds, especially a loud hiss when you get too near the bird, along with grunts! Also the wings emit a loud, vibrational sound in flight, thought to be a contact call. The word Swan derives from the Anglo-Saxon meaning sounder, probably referring to the swishing sound of its wings made whilst flying. The term 'swan song' arose in ancient Greece to represent a final effort made just before death (or lately, a final performance e.g. in the theatre) based on the belief that the Swan sang a beautiful song just before dying, having been silent all its life. Although not wholly true the fable has entered popular mythology. The adult male is called a cob from the Middle English cobbe, meaning leader of a group, the adult female is a pen and the young are called cygnets, from the French cygnus for Swan with the diminutive suffix –et added. The Mute Swan is one of the heaviest flying birds, weighing 12 kg.. The oldest living Mute Swan recorded was 27 years 6 months old. Swan Vestas adopted the Mute Swan as a logo on it match boxes, using an Eric Hosking photograph.

The Mute Swan has long been a royal bird. Edward I used the Swan as a badge. Edward III passed protective legislation as the bird was valued as a table bird for eating. Henry VII imposed fines for stealing their eggs. The Crown still has the right to Swans on the Thames from London Bridge to Henley. The bills are marked with a nick by officials from the Vintner's and Dyer's Livery Companies. The Swan's popularity if reflected in the fact that 'The Swan' is the fifth most popular pub name in Britain and 'The White Swan' is the 38th most popular. Swans remain paired for life and practice sexual monogamy, which is rare in the world of birds. The Mute Swan was voted the national bird Denmark in 1984 by TV viewers. The first written record of the name in English dates from the 8th century.

The **Nightingale**'s formal name comes from the German nachtingal which means night songstress, making the historical mistake that it is the female that sings. In English the word became nyghtgale and thence to Nightingale. The Mid English word gale means to sing which the bird does exceptionally well! The first written record of the English name for the Nightingale dates from the 685 AD.

The jar in the **Nightjar**'s name formerly meant a quivering or grating sound rather than today's meaning of discordant. Their nocturnal song disturbed or jarred people's sleep.

The **Nuthatch**'s name derives from the bird's habit of placing nuts in

the gaps of bark and using its bill to open them i.e. hatch them. The German name is nussbrecher, meaning nut breaker.

Qi The name **Osprey** comes from the Old French osfraie and the Latin ossifraga, which means bone breaker from the manner in which the Osprey takes fish and eats them. The Osprey was driven to extinction in 1916 due to persecution for taking fish, egg collection and being killed for display. It returned naturally in 1954 and slowly re-colonised first in Scotland and then in England and Wales, with the help of re-introduction schemes, such as the one at Rutland Water in the 1990's. Osprey numbers have increased over the last 25 years by about 450%, according to the Rare Breeding Birds Panel (in 2014) to about 220 breeding pairs. The bird differs from other birds of prey and is in a separate family, Pandionidae. Its toes are of equal length and the outer toe can turn backwards so there are two forward facing and two rear facing toes, which enables the bird to skilfully grab fish from the surface of water. The lower surface of its toes are covered in spicules (needles) to help them grasp their fish prey. A pair need to catch about 400 fish in a breeding season and they have about a 1 in 4 fishing success rate. One interesting piece of folklore is that the bird has such extraordinary powers that they are able to make fish turn over in the water and show their white undersides, making them much easier to see and catch. The first written record of the name in English dates from the 10th century.

Qi The meaning of **Peregrine** derives from 'the wanderer from abroad' (as does the more general word, peregrination), originally an animal that has travelled 'per agrum', i.e. through fields. In World War 2 a law was passed allowing the bird to be culled as it was catching carrier Pigeons and so hampering the war effort. Numbers recovered after the war only for them to decline in the 1950's due to the pesticide DDT causing thin egg shells (see Section 'Local and common names' under Sparrowhawk Page 46). Happily they have recovered again and they breed (amongst other places) in city centres, nesting in tall buildings, where the Pigeon population provides easy meals for the birds. The highest density of breeding Peregrine in the world is found in New York city, where the bird has adapted to city life.

The **Pochard**'s formal name comes from the French pocher meaning to poke - whilst feeding.

The **Ptarmigan**'s name comes from the Gaelic tarmanchan meaning croaker i.e. the name is onomatopoeic. The Ptarmigan is unique in being the only bird to have four seasonal plumages. The male is 25% heavier than the 400 g female.

Qi The **Puffin**'s name is the result of a muddle that existed for many years, with confusion arising between the names for the Puffin and the Manx Shearwater. The two birds are not at all similar! Juvenile Manx Shearwater were caught and killed for food and the name Puffin was given to the cured carcass of the bird, which was corpulent or puffed, hence puffin. The name Mank Puffin was given to the Manx Shearwater originally and is established in the Latin name for the bird, *Puffinus puffinus*. Later the name Puffin was acquired by the bird we now know as the Puffin, which also has a puffed out belly.

Qi The name **Raven** comes from the Old Norse mythological bird god hrafnagud, translated into the Old English hraefn and thence to Raven (see Page 143). The first written record of the English name dates from c. 699 AD. The Raven is the largest Corvid in the Corvidae family and the largest perching bird in the world. It is also one of the most widespread birds in the world, capable of living from low levels to high altitudes and in many different climates, from desert to frozen arctic steppe. The Raven appears in the mythology of many cultures and

some examples are given later. The Raven is the national bird of Bhutan and represents the Guardian deity, Jarog Dongchen. The Raven was persecuted in the countryside for it predatory habits, not least the gruesome habit of pecking the eyes out of victims, and bounties were paid to have it killed. In towns and cities it was protected, as it cleaned up the dirty streets. Hardy recorded that two Ravens smelt a hearse as it passed and swooped onto the coffin. An English folk song entitled 'Twa corbies' is based on two Ravens feeding on a dead soldier's body. The Raven breeds very early in the year enabling it to feed off carrion such as still-born lambs and placentas. As members of the Corvid family (Covidae) they are highly intelligent birds. In one experiment Ravens were able to recognise individual voices of other Ravens and they reacted to the voice as either a friend or an invader. They also had a good long term memory for these voices. The Raven is one of only two British birds that are capable of nesting in winter.

The name **Redstart** is not entirely accurate as the tail of this bird is a prominent orange colour rather than red. As with the Robin, the word orange was not part of the English language until after the name for this

bird had been established. The word start is also an old name for tail. Aristotle observed that the Redstart was not seen in winter and postulated that it turned into a Robin!

The ring in the **Ring Ouzel**'s name derives from the male's clear white crescent shaped band across its chest. The female has a less prominent chest band and the juveniles have none. The second word comes from the Old English name for the Blackbird, osel and then to ousel and finally ouzel. Ring Ouzel numbers have decreased over the last 25 years by about 72%, according to the Rare Breeding Birds Panel report (in 2014).

Qi The name **Robin** is derived from a pet name for the human name Robert. This accords with the familiarity that the Robin has with humans, being a frequent visitor to gardens and bird feeders. The first written record of the English name Robin was about the year 530 AD. In the 1960's a vote, published in The Times, appointed the Robin as the national bird. In 2015 a national poll again voted the Robin as the national bird. In fact the Robin is very aggressive and will fight furiously to protect its territory. The sexes are identical. The female sings in autumn, probably to denote her feeding territory. The average life span is just over one year. The Robin was the ninth most common bird observed in the Big Garden Birdwatch 2013.

Qi The name **Ruff** technically only applies to the male bird. The female is called a Reeve. The male (who weighs 180 g) is larger than the female (weighing 110 g), being typical for a polygamous bird which has to engage in an intense sexual selection process. The male's cloacal organ is also comparatively large. Ruff obviously derives from the ornate collar of feathers that the male acquires in breeding plumage. Males with highly coloured ruffs are called territorial males and they stake out a small patch on the lek, where they engage in a vigorous display ritual in order to attract and mate with a female. A small proportion of males have a lighter coloured ruff and they are satellite males, who stand on the outer part of the lek. They are opportunistic maters, running to a female whilst the other males are not looking! Ruffs start their winter moult before migrating to winter in Kenya, with the males moulting before the females. Ruffs also have an intermediate moult between winter and summer. Siberian Ruffs undertake a migratory flight of up to 18000 miles. The word Reeve is possibly associated with the ornate clothing of an official's robes and was used in the 15th and 16th century for both male and female birds. The word Ruff was brought into use in the 17th century and then was adopted for naming just the male bird. Some sources associate the bird with the item of clothing by the same name, others disagree stating the item of clothing comes from ruffle, meaning wrinkled or folded.

The **Sanderling**'s name is simply made up of 'sand' plus two suffixes - '-er' and '-ling'. The bird breeds in the high Arctic and migrates all the way to West Africa, stopping off in Britain to refuel. The bird gains weight by laying down fat for its long journey, increasing its weight from 50 g to 80 g, giving it enough fuel for almost a 3000 km journey.

The **Scaup**'s formal English name links to the duck's food, with skalp meaning mussel bed.

The name **Serin** comes from the French for Canary. The Serin appears to have no native English names.

The name **Shag** derives from the tuft seen on the bird's head in the breeding season. This was used to differentiate the Shag from the Cormorant although the names are often inter-changeable in other countries.

Snipe dervies from the Middle English snite and the Old Norse myrisnipa - a mire snipe. The German snipon means a long, thin object.

Starling

Qi The **Starling** is a familiar bird, although numbers have fallen in recent years. The name is comprised of star, from the Old English stare and refers to the juvenile's starry plumage plus the suffix –ling. In winter numbers are supplemented by migrants from the continent forming huge flocks; some are estimated to exceed 1 million birds. At evening they gather to roost, performing magnificent displays as they fall into bushes (or buildings like Brighton pier) for the night. Starlings are expert mimics and reproduce the songs of other birds and even the alarm and 'phone sounds they hear. In 1890 Eugene Schieffelen introduced 60 European Starlings into New York's Central Park (up until then it was absent in the USA) because the bird was mentioned by Shakespeare! The bird readily took to its new country and eventually became a pest and was subject to control measures to limit numbers. The Starling, like many birds, changes its diet with the seasons. In summer the bird eats soil invertebrates, like crane-fly larvae (leatherjackets) and in winter switches to a plant based diet. In doing so its intestine increases in length to cope with digesting this food.

The word **Smew** possibly derives from small, being the smallest saw-tooth in the family Mergini.

Qi The name **Swallow** derives from the Mid English swalowe and the Germanic swalwo, which means cleft stick, referring to the Swallow's forked tail. The first written record of the English name Swallow dates from c.685 AD. Incidentally the forked tail is present only on adult birds. If you see Swallows flocking in autumn, ready for their perilous long migration journey to South Africa, many birds will not have tail streamers and these are the juveniles. The male's tail feathers are about 20% longer than the female's, these being used by the male to attract a mate. However, this is not all good news, as it takes more energy to produce longer feathers and it reduces manoeuvrability.

Swallows work very hard to make a nest and feed young. A new nest contains up to 1400 pellets of mud and one nest examined contained 1635 rootlets, 139 pine needles and 450 pieces of dried grass. The birds can make 100 trips a day covering 137 miles nest building, taking about a week to 10 days. In an experiment a Swallow's eggs were taken away as soon as they were laid. The bird went on to lay 19 eggs instead of the normal 5. The brood patch has touch sensors which count the number of eggs laid and it tells the bird when to stop laying. If there are too few eggs the bird carries on laying! Each brood will consume 150 000 insects up to fledging at about 21 days. Swallow numbers have increased over the last 40 years (Breeding Bird Survey to 2012) by 20%. The oldest living Swallow recorded was 11 years 1 month old.

Qi The **Swift** flies quickly but it is not the fastest bird in level flight. Its close relative the Spine-tailed Swift takes that honour with a top level flight speed of 105 mph. Of the British birds, the Eider holds the record for the fastest constant level flight at 47 mph. (The Peregrine is the fastest bird (in the world) reaching speeds of around 300 km / hr but that is in a burst of vertical, stoop flight). The Swift we see flies at around 40 km / hr and can reach above 80 km / hr in a burst of speed, for example when trying to impress a potential mate. The word Swift comes from the Old English swifan, meaning moving fast. The Swift also flies immense distances. One estimate is that if a bird flies 500 miles a day, a 7 year old bird will fly 1.28 million miles.

Swedish researchers fitted geolocators to several Swifts and recovered 19 of them. The data showed that three of the birds never rested and all the birds were in the air 99% of the time (except when nesting). Swifts also make a long ascent to altitudes of 3km, often at twilight. They can sleep on the wing. A French airman in the 1914-18 war was gliding down behind enemy lines when at 10,000 feet he found himself amongst a flock of motionless Swifts.

Swifts fly considerable distances from their nest sites to feed. Mysteriously, they can detect a cold weather front a considerable distance away (with a concentration of flies ahead of it) and will fly there to feed. One radar tracking showed them moving from London to the North Sea off the Lincolnshire coast. Very unusually for birds the young are able to slip into torpor and survive for up to 5 days waiting for the returning adults. The only other birds able to slip into a torpid state are the Hummingbirds. Swift numbers have decreased by 38% over the last 25 years (to 2012).

The **Teal** has a name which is not used as a word in any other context, except it is used as the name of a colour, from the bright green speculum on the wing of the Teal. The name is onomatopoeic from the Old English tel, representing the chuckling sound of a feeding bird. The Teal is Britain's smallest duck.

Qi The name of the **Turtle Dove** is onomatopoeic from its soft turr-turr song, so redolent of bygone summer's days. The name derives from the French name for the bird, tourterelle. The number of Turtle Doves in Britain has dropped dramatically, by as much as 93%, over the past

40 years, with numbers dropping on the continent as well. Possible reasons include changes in agricultural practice where there are fewer weed seeds, especially fumitory, for the birds to feed on. It is the only migratory Dove (or Pigeon – the same Columbidae family) and might be suffering from loss of habitat in its winter quarters. The bird is still shot (illegally) on its migratory journey, reducing numbers still further.

The derivation of rail in the **Water Rail**'s names is from the French word rale, which is a death rattle, linked to bird's scraping noise.

Qi On the face of it the name **Wheatear** implies the bird eats wheat and there is something significant about its ear. Neither is true! The words wheat and ear are 16th century corruptions of white and arse (the latter word was not vulgar at the time) referring to the white rump, which is prominent in both the male and the female bird. The Wheatear undertakes the longest migratory journey of any songbird i.e. in the order Passeriformes. The Wheatear was once caught in large numbers for the table. Nooses were used to catch the birds but catching such numbers must have been difficult as the Wheatear does not form flocks. Gilbert White noted that the bird "appeared at the table of all the gentry that entertain with any degree of elegance". Daniel Defoe recorded that they tasted delicious.

Qi The **Wigeon**'s name is onomatopoeic from the Latin vibionem which translated later into wigene and thence to Wigeon. The Wigeon has a very distinctive whistle which is redolent of bird-watching in winter over estuarine mud-flats, where the bird gathers in large flocks, constantly whistling. Folk lore has it that Wigeon are the souls of unchristened babies, from the sad sound of their whistle. The oldest living Wigeon recorded was 34 years 7 months old.

The **Winchat**'s name refers to its habitat, with whin- being an old word for gorse and -chat from the call sound it makes.

Qi The **Woodcock** certainly lives in woods but the male and female are virtually identical, so there is no clear reason for the second part of the name, cock. Historically they were given separate name i.e. wuduhona for the male and wuduhana for the female. The first written record of the English name for the Woodcock dates from the 8th century. Woodcock is used as a word for a simpleton and refers to the ease with which the bird is caught. It is so well camouflaged that the bird can be caught on the nest. However, there is proof that if a nesting female is disturbed she can carry one of her fledglings off as she flies away. The Woodcock was once eaten in large numbers. In the 13th century the market price of a Woodcock was fixed at a penny half-penny (and a Pheasant at 4 pennies). It was caught using a mesh erected in the woods where they lived, called a cock-shoot. The male's twilight display flight is called a roding. The Woodcock is one of the few birds which can see through 360 degrees, with its eyes set either side of its head. One very strange use of a bird's feather is in the production of Rolls Royce cars where they use a Woodcock's pin feather to paint the stripe down the side of the car!

The British population of Woodcock is increased by migrants from Scandinavia in winter. In the 16th century there was speculation in northern counties that the Woodcock's absence in summer was due to the fact that it flew to the moon! This debate continued for 200 years! Numbers have declined by 74% in the last 40 years (to 2011).

Qi The **Woodpigeon** is seen in many locations not just woods. The word Pigeon derives from the Latin pipire (to chirp) through the Old French pijon to the English pigeon. The first written record of the English name for Woodpigeon dates from c.685 AD. The word also means someone who is easily cheated linked to the phrase stool pigeon, coming from the use of the Woodpigeon as a decoy in falconry. Licences are still issued to shoot this bird, which is seen as a pest for eating crops. For many centuries the bird has been caught for food. The breast muscle accounts for 40% of the bird's weight, hence the common use of Pigeon breasts in cooking. The names Pigeon and Dove are interchangeable; Pigeon derives from French and Dove from the Anglo-Saxon. The bird's close relative is called the Rock Dove. The Woodpigeon is one of the few British birds that potentially can breed throughout the year. The male and female are both capable of mating at any time of the year. By contrast in almost all other birds both the male's and female's sexual apparatus (the gonads) shrinks to save weight meaning they cannot mate. Unusually Pigeons are able to suck up water when drinking as opposed to most other birds who have to fill their mouths and then tip their heads up to take in water.

SCIENTIFIC NAMES

The third category of name that is used to identify a bird is its scientific name. Scientists, naturalists and collectors saw the need to have a specific name for every species of bird (and by extension all living things in the natural world) which is a unique identifier. Clearly local names are of no use as they vary a great deal over time and place and often are inaccurate. Alongside the need for an agreed formal English name (as discussed above) attempts were made to produce a global naming system which would provide a unique identifier as well as tell us something about the creature or organism being named.

Aristotle (384 – 322BC) was a keen observer of nature, including birds, and he named the birds he saw, some of which contribute to the names we use today, especially scientific names. Pliny the Elder (23 – 79AD) also added to the fund of knowledge at the time, writing a book, the *Naturalis Historia*, which compiled all that was known at the time on natural history. Again, this was a major contribution for the time and informed the naming of some birds. The earliest extant writings in Britain date from the 6th century from records left by St. Serf and St. Columba. The first attempt to list British birds was made in the 16th century by Turner. He listed 110 birds. Gesner produced a structured list later in the 16th century and Merritt published a list in the 17th century. The first major influential work was written by Ray in 1676, with a major contribution by his friend Willughby, who sadly died before the work was completed. The book contained the results of the scientific examination of birds, such as dissection, with a first attempt to classify birds scientifically. This was followed by books by Pennant (a friend of Gilbert White of Selbourne fame) in the 18th century. Each successive work contained more birds in greater detail as our knowledge of birds grew.

The major breakthrough in designating a unique name for all living things came with the work of Carl von Linne, a Swedish naturalist who also worked in Holland. Given that he is remembered for his Latin based naming system, he is best known by the Latinate name Carolus Linnaeus. His speciality was botany but he had a wide interest in the natural world. Linnaeus published the first edition of his *Systema Naturae* in 1735 and produced the last and 10th edition in 1758, covering plants as well as animals. He proposed a binary nomenclature system as the basis for a unique name. The first word would relate to the genus of the bird (explained in the next paragraph) and the second word would be an adjective, which in combination would provide a name exclusive to that bird. The words in the name are Latin but do not necessarily originate from Latin. In fact many of the scientific names of birds derive from other languages including Greek, German, Dutch, Norwegian. The binary system is used today and has been adopted internationally.

Birds (as with all living things) are divided into a hierarchy or taxonomy which classifies birds into groupings according to some pre-defined common characteristics. With around 10 000 bird species in the world clearly this is a very large group and needs to be split into smaller groupings. Some birds are closely related in their evolutionary history, others are further apart. The hierarchy works down from the class of aves, which includes all 10 000 birds (using the simple definition that all birds have feathers!). This is then split into 28 orders, then into 172 families, followed by genera, and finally species, which are the individual bird (setting aside the complication of races and sub-species - see next page). So for example, the Robin is clearly a bird, it is in the order Passeriformes (basically a perching bird, but that is simplistic), the family Turdidae (containing the Chats and Thrushes and Nightingales), the genus Erithacus and finally the species Robin. The scientific name for the Robin is *Erithacus rubecula*, with the word *Erithacus* simply meaning Robin and *rubecula* deriving from the Latin for red. No other bird has this scientific name and when this name is used it uniquely identifies the bird whose formal English name is Robin. Whilst there are other species of Robin in the world they have a different scientific name.

The writing convention is that the first letter of the first word is upper case, the rest is in lower case and in scientific works the letters are italicised. When a genus name is repeated in the same passage of text, the name is abbreviated to the first letter of the genus name. In a text on Thrushes, for example, the first reference to a Thrush, say Fieldfare would be *Turdus pilarus* but a subsequent reference to Blackbird would be written as *T. merula*. Where the species is not clear, say from a difficult observation, the genus name is given followed by (non-italicised) sp.. This might occur with long distance views of Terns and this would be written as *Sterna* sp..

However, scientific names are not fixed forever. Scientists are using more sophisticated techniques, particularly DNA analysis, and this leads to birds being re-classified as closer relatives are identified. As a consequence the Robin has been re-classified into the Flycatcher family of Muscicapinae but maintains its genus Erithacus within that family.

A complication arises with sub-species of birds, which are given a tri-nomial name. With a number of species of birds variations occur within the species, often geographical variations. Each sub-species retains the same binomial species name but a third word is added to provide a separate identification for the sub-species. So for example, the species scientific name for the Yellow Wagtail is *Motacilla flava* but there are many sub-species, the main differences being in the head feather pattern. One bird, referred to as the nominate species, is given the repetitive third word, so for the **Yellow Wagtail** the nominate species is called *Motacilla flava flava*. The other sub-species are then given a trinomial name based on this. Hence, the sub-species names for the Yellow Wagtail include *Motacilla flava thunbergi*, *Motacilla flava feldegg* and *Motacilla flava cinereocapilla*.

Scientific bird names

The rest of this section will examine the origin of a selection of British birds' scientific names. Once again this gives a fascinating insight into the life of the bird, the tales and myths that surround it, the results of human interaction with the bird and its characteristics and behaviour. The list is in alphabetical order of the formal English name, consistent with previous sections, to make referencing easier. Some have been grouped together where sensible and to avoid repetition e.g. Swans.

The tale of the **Arctic Skua**'s local name dung bird, explained earlier, is incorporated into the scientific name *Stercorarius parasiticus* with *Stercorarius* deriving from stercus for dung and arius belonging to. This also applies to the **Great Skua** whose scientific name is *Stercorarius skua*. The second name *skua* comes from the Faroe Islanders' name for the bird. The **Pomarine Skua** shares the first word of its scientific name with the Arctic Skua i.e. *Stercoraruis*. The second part of the its name is *pomarinus* from the Greek pomato for lid and rhinos for nose.

The **Arctic Tern**'s scientific name is *Sternus paradiaea* with *Sternus* from the Old English strearn for tern and *paradiaea* meaning paradise. The first part of the **Black Tern**'s scientific name *Chlidonias niger* refers to the former English name for Terns as sea swallows. The name *Chlidonias* comes from the Greek khelidon for swallow and –ios for like, along with the Latin *niger* for black. The **Common Tern** has the name *Sternus hirundo* with *hirundo* from hirundine, being the common family name for the Swallows and Martins. This links again with the local names for the bird, such as sea swallow and shear tail. The **Little Tern**'s scientific name is *Sternula albifrons* with *albifrons* meaning white brow, being a clear identification feature of the bird.

Qi The **Roseate Tern**'s scientific name of *Sterna dougallii* is unusual in that it incorporates a person's name. Dr. Peter McDougall first identified the bird in 1812, having shot one and sent it to Montagu (of Harrier fame) for identification. Numbers of this bird have fluctuated. Formerly it was caught for its feathers for use in the millinery trade and for taxidermy. In its winter quarters in Senegal and Ghana the bird is still caught as food. Roseate Terns leave their breeding colonies and gather in Dublin Bay before making their migratory journey to West Africa. In what is rare behaviour for a Tern, the Roseate Tern is a kleptoparasite, stealing food from other fish-eating birds such as Puffin. It is thought they do this when the seas are rough as plunge diving Terns cannot catch fish in turbulent waters whilst diving birds like Puffin can still catch fish, which the Tern then tries to steal.

Finally in this group of Terns the **Sandwich Tern**'s scientific name is *Sterna sanvicensis* referring to the place Sandwich, where a specimen was shot to identify the bird.

The **Avocet**'s scientific name is *Recurvirostra avosetta* with recurvus meaning bent back and rostris being the bill plus avosetta, a Venetian name for the bird associated with lawyer's traditional dress. Also *avosetta* comes from the Latin avis for bird plus a diminutive ending indicating charm and grace rather than small.

Qi The strange derivation of the English name **Barnacle Goose** was explained earlier. The scientific name for the bird is *Branta leucopsis* with *Branta* deriving from brandgas meaning burnt Goose and *leucopsis* is white faced. An interesting question was posed relating to the physical training of the young geese who have to fly a long way very soon after they are first able to fly. The Goose breeds in Greenland and Svalbard and these populations fly to the Hebrides and Solway Firth respectively. The young have no time to train or build up their muscles yet they set off and complete an epic 2 500 km journey without any preparatory training. How?

The **Barn Owl**'s scientific name is *Tyto alba* with *Tyto* meaning owl and *alba* white - very apt name!

The **Bar-tailed Godwit**'s scientific name *Limosa lapponica* is again aptly named, with *Limosa* meaning mud, where it is found feeding and *lapponica* from Lapland, where it breeds. Its close cousin the **Balck-tailed Godwit** has the repetitive name *Limosa limosa*.

All three Swans that can be seen in Britain belong to the genus Cygnus, which simply means Swan. The word derives from Greek mythology, as detailed later in the Section 'Some common mythological stories'. **Bewick's Swan** is named after Bewick, an early ornithologist and bird illustrator, born in 1753. The Bewick's Swan's scientific name, *Cygnus columbianus,* is named after the Columbia river in North America. The **Mute Swan**, our only indigenous Swan, is named *Cygnus olor* which merely repeats Swan in Latin. Finally, the **Whooper Swan** also has a repetitive name *Cygnus cygnus.* The Bewick's Swan and the Whooper Swan both breed in high northern latitudes on Arctic tundra and migrate south in family groups as winter approaches. The Whooper Swan flies at 2500 m at a speed of 88 km/hr covering over 1000 km in 12 hours in a temperature of - 40° C - some journey!. The Whooper swan was nominated the national bird Finland in 1981.

The bills of these birds have varying amounts of yellow at the base and black at the tip. Birds can be individually identified by the distinctive pattern of colour on their bill. Both have distinctive calls compared to the almost silent Mute Swan.

The **Bean Goose**'s scientific name is *Anser fabalis* which comes from *anser* for goose and *fabalis* meaning of beans (from its diet).

The **Bittern**'s scientific name is *Botaurus stellaris* with *botaurus* made up of bos meaning bull and taurus also bull! *Stellaris* is Latin for starry, referring to the bird's mottled plumage. In fact the formal English name also derives from the same source as *botaurus.*

Qi The scientific name for the **Black Grouse** has its roots in the records made by Aristotle who mentioned a ground bird, giving it the name tetrix. The scientific name is *Tetrao tetrix* which repeats gamebird and ground bird. Not very descriptive! The bird has a distinctive courtship ritual. At dawn in spring the males strut around a traditional area called a lek and display whilst making a highly distinctive mating call. In western Europe these gatherings seldom involve more than 40 birds; in Russia 150 is not uncommon and 200 have been recorded. The bird's tail feathers have been popular adornments in hats worn with Highland dress, most commonly associated with Glengarry and Balmoral or Tam O'Shanter caps. They still continue to be worn by pipers of civilian and military pipe bands. Since 1904 all ranks of the Royal Scot's and King's Own Scottish Borderers have worn them in their full-dress headgear.

The **Black Guillemot's** name is *Cepphus grylle* which comes from the Greek kepphus for a waterbird described by Aristotle and the Swedish grissla meaning guillemot. This illustrates how words from two different languages (Greek and Swedish) are Latinised. The **Guillemot**'s name is *Uria aalge* which comes from the Greek ouriaa a water bird mentioned by Athenaeus and the Danish aalge meaning auk (from the Old Norwegian alka).

The **Black Redstart**'s scientific name confuses the colours of its prominent tail with the name *Phoenicurus ochruros*. *Phoenicurus* is Greek for crimson tail and *ochruros* also Greek for pale yellow tail. In fact crimson is more apt.

The family name of Thrushes, Turdidae, simply means Thrush. Members include the **Blackbird**,*Turdus merula*, with Turdidae being the family name for thrushes and *merula* for black; the **Fieldfare**, *Turdus pilaris*, with *pilaris* meaning Thrush as well; the **Mistle Thrush** *Turdus viscivorus,* with *viscivorus* from the Latin viscum for mistletoe and vorare to devour (the bird does eat mistletoe!); the **Redwing**, *Turdus iliacus*, with *iliacus* referring to the flanks, which are red; the **Ring Ouzel** *Turdus torquatus*, deriving from torquis Latin for collar (prominent white on the male) and the **Song Thrush**, *Turdus philomelos*. The second part of the name, *philomelos*, is based on a Greek myth that Philomena was turned into a nightingale and sang a lover's song.

Another genus with several members is the **Sylvia Warblers**, with sylvia referring to woods, where the birds are found. The group includes the **Blackcap**, *Sylvia atricapilla,* with *Sylvia* meaning wood and *atri* for black and *capilla* for cap; **Dartford Warbler**, *Sylvia undata*, with *undata* meaning wavy, the only bird of this group that is an all-year resident in Britain (the Blackcaps and Chiffchaffs seen in winter are likely to be migrants from the continent); the **Garden Warbler**, *Sylvia borin* with *borin* being Italian for a warbler; the **Lesser Whitethroat**, *Sylvia curruca* and the **Whitethroat** *Sylvia communis* with *communis* meaning common, as in ordinary rather than numerous.

The family of Gulls (Laridae) include the **Black-headed Gull** with the complex name of *Chroicocephalus ridibundus* which comes from Greek kroikos for coloured and kephale for head (true only in summer) and the Latin ridere plus abundare meaning abounds or abundant. Other members of this family include the **Common Gull**, which is in the Larus genus with *Larus* simply meaning seabird. Oddly whilst Gulls are synonymous with the seaside they are not particularly pelagic birds i.e. birds that live on the sea like, for example, Kittiwakes that only come ashore to breed. The scientific name for the Common Gull is *Larus canus* with *canus* meaning grey. The North American name for this bird is Mew Gull, with mew being used generically for Gull in some British local names. Others birds in this genus with the first name *Larus* include **Audouin's Gull**, *Larus audouinii*, Audouin was a 19th century French scientist who worked on all aspects of natural science; the **Glaucous Gull** *Larus hyperboreus*, with *hyperboreus* meaning over the north; the **Great Black-backed Gull**, *Larus marinus*, *marinus* meaning marine; the **Herring Gull**, *Larus argentatus*, *argentatus* meaning ornamented with silver (*argent*); the **Lesser Black-backed Gull**, *Larus fuscus*, *fuscus* meaning dusky; the **Little Gull**, *Larus minutus*, *minutus* meaning small and the **Mediterranean Gull**, *Larus melanocephalus* with melas meaning black and kephalos head (but only in its summer plumage).

Qi The scientific name *Podiceps nigricollis* for the **Black-necked Grebe** reflects the bird's evolutionary journey. *Podiceps* is a combination of the Latin podex for anus and pes for foot. Birds in this

family of Podicipedidae have adapted so well to water that their feet have gradually moved backwards which makes them excellent swimmers (above and below water) but clumsy on land. The Black-necked Grebe remains flightless for up to 10 months of the year and then flies for up to 6000 km on a migratory journey! *Nigricollis* comes from the Latin niger for black and collis for neck. The **Great Crested Grebe** has the name *Podiceps cristatus* with *cristatus* meaning simply crest. Similarly the **Red-necked Grebe**'s scientific name is *Podiceps grisegena* with *grisegena* oddly meaning grey cheeks rather than referring to the more distinctive red neck. The **Slavonian Grebe**'s scientific name is *Podiceps auritus* with *auritus* meaning ear, referring to the prominent head feathers (except they are not ear feathers) which are highly prominent in breeding plumage. The Great Crested Grebe was another bird that was almost driven to extinction in the 19th century as a result of being shot for its feathers to satisfy the demand of the millinery trade. By 1860 a count revealed only 42 breeding pairs left in Britain. The Bird Protection Acts helped restore the bird's fortunes. By the late 1880's groups of ladies joined together to campaign against the use of bird feathers. These groups instigated the formation of the Society for the Protection of Birds, later the RSPB.

The only British Grebe that does not have the genus name *Podiceps* is the **Little Grebe**, whose scientific name is *Tachybaptus ruficollis*, with *Tachybaptus* coming from the Greek takhos meaning fast and bapto to sink, reflecting how quickly the bird dives when even slightly disturbed. *Ruficollis* is from the Latin rufus reddish and collus neck. Again, a simple and clear description of the nature of this bird.

The **Blue Tit**'s scientific name emphasises the bird's colour as in *Cyanistes caeruleus* from the Latin cyaneus for dark-blue and caeruleus

Willow Tit

meaning blue. Other species in the Paridae family inclue the **Coal Tit** whose name is *Periparus ater* which comes from peri and parus meaning very much a tit and ater for black. The **Crested Tit**'s name is *Lophophanes cristatus* which is from the Greek lophos for crest and phanes meaning light and the Latin crista for crest. The scientific name for the **Great Tit** simply repeats the same as in *Parus major* i.e. the Latin *Parus* for tit and *major* for great. Easy! The **Marsh Tit**'s name is *Poecile palustris* from the Greek poikolos for spotted and palus, a marsh. Here it is seen in bushes and trees rather than marshes. The final bird in this group is the **Willow Tit,** with the scientific name *Poecile montana* from the Greek poikolos for spotted and the Latin montanus for mountaineer, where it is seen in Europe as it migrates. In Britain it is sedentary and is seen, like its close relative the Marsh Tit, in bushes and trees rather than on mountain tops. Marsh Tit numbers have fallen by 44% over the last 40 years (to 2012) and the Willow Tit by 76%, one of the highest declines recorded for a breeding bird. The **Long-tailed Tit** is in the Aegithalidae family and has the scientific name *Aegithalos caudatus* which comes from the Greek aigithalos for a tit and Latin cauda for tail.

The scientific name for the **Brambling** derives from a description of a bird made by Aristophanes, who lived 446 – 386 BC. The name survived in Greek as phrugilos and then into Latin as fringilla. This illustrates the long history of some of our bird names. The Brambling's scientific name is *Fringilla montifringilla*, with monti- simply meaning mountain. The Brambling is sometimes described as the Scandinavian Chaffinch. Numbers migrating here in winter vary depending on the availability of their favourite food, beech mast. Even in their winter plumage Brambling are colourful.

The **Brent Goose** has two forms that are seen in Britain. The dark-bellied form, which winters in England and breeds in Siberia, has the scientific name *Branta bernicla bernicla* making this the nominate species. The pale-bellied sub-species *Branta bernicla horta* breeds in Greenland and over winters in Ireland and Scotland. The north American form, the Black Brant, is considered a separate species, *Branta nigricans* and is a rare visitor to Britain. The **Canada Goose,** *Branta canadensis* comes from brandgas meaning burnt goose and *canadensis*, Canada.

The scientific name of the **Bullfinch** is *Pyrrhula pyrrhula* which comes from the Greek purrohulas which is a worm-eating bird mentioned by Aristotle.

The **Buzzard**'s scientific name is *Buteo buteo* which simply repeats the name Buzzard twice!

The **Capercaillie**'s scientific name is *Tetrao urogallus* which comes from the Greek tetraon, being a type of gamebird and the German auerhuhn meaning mountain cock plus the Latin gallus, cock.

Qi The **Cattle Egret**'s scientific name is *Bubulcus ibis* with *Bubulcus* coming from the Latin for herdsman. The Cattle Egret is one of the few birds found on every continent of the world. The bird is popular with herdsmen as it rids their cattle of parasites. *Ibis* is not accurate as the Egret is closely related to Herons (the Ardeidae family) not Ibis, which are in a different family (with the rather complex name Threskionithidae).

The **Carrion Crow** is in the Corvidae family and some members of this family share the same initial scientific name, *Corvus*, meaning Crow. This word derives from the Latin word for an iron bar used as a grappling hook, now linked to the English word crowbar. The Carrion Crow's full name is *Corvus corone* with *corone* being repetitive, as corone is Greek for Crow. Other members of the family with scientific names beginning with *Corvus* are **Jackdaw**, *Corvus monedula* with *monedula* repetitive being the Latin for Jackdaw; **Raven** is another repetitive name in *Corvus corax* with *corax* the Greek for Raven and finally **Rook**, *Corvus frugilegus* with *frugilegus* deriving from frugis meaning fruit and legere to lift. The bird is vegetarian, though not exclusively so.

Qi The **Chaffinch** is a member of the Fringilldae family, so it shares

its initial name *Fringilla* with the Brambling (above) plus the Latin *coelebs*, meaning bachelor. The Chaffinch was given its scientific name by Linnaeus himself in Sweden. He correctly observed that in winter the male birds were seen in flocks with no females. The females migrate, often to Britain, where female only flocks can be seen. The males stay behind, as bachelors, and are able to set up new breeding territories early in spring to await the female's return later from their winter quarters. When males arrive at the breeding site first it is called protandry. It is not unusual amongst birds for males and females to go their separate ways after mating, some re-establishing pair bonds on their separate return to the breeding site. For example, Puffins and Guillemots do this with the return accompanied by a flamboyant re-bonding ceremony.

The **Chiffchaff** is in the genus Phylloscopus which derives from the Greek phullion for leaf and skopos for watcher. In spring that is where the bird is seen, moving quickly amongst the newly emerged leaves in the tree canopy, picking off small insects as it goes, with the male stopping frequently to emit its loud and distinctive song. The Chiffchaff's scientific name is *Phylloscopus collybita*, with *collybita* from the Greek for money-changer (the bird's song apparently sounding like money being counted). Other members of this genus include a bird that looks very much like the Chiffchaff, but has a distinctly different and tuneful song, the **Willow Warbler**. This bird's scientific name is *Phylloscopus trochilus* with *trochilus* referring to a bird mentioned by Arisotle. The other member is the **Wood Warbler**, *Phylloscopus sibilatrix* from the Latin sibilare to whistle, referring to the bird's lovely song. Numbers of this bird have dropped by 62% in the 14 years to 2009.

The **Chough** is a member of the Corvidae family and has the scientific name *Pyrrohcorax pyrrohcorax*, from the Greek purrhos meaning flame-coloured, alluding to its bright red bill, and korax meaning Raven (a member of the same Corvidae family).

The name *Emberiza* merely means Bunting. This family includes the **Cirl Bunting** *Emberiza cirlus* - with *cirlus* an Italian name for the bird; the **Corn Bunting** - *Emberiza calandra* which confuses the bird with the distinctly different Calandra Lark; the **Reed Bunting** has the cumbersome scientific name of *Emberiza schoeniclus* with *schoeniclus* means reed dwelling and finally the **Yellowhammer** - *Emberiza citrinella* with *citrinella* meaning citrus tree alluding to the bird's yellow coloration.

Qi The **Collared Dove**'s scientific name is *Streptopelia decaocto*. Streptos is collar and peleia is Dove which accords with the bird's appearance. The second word comes from Greek mythology with *deca* meaning ten and *octo* eight which refer to a folk story involving the call of a bird sent to rescue a poorly paid servant girl. The Collared Dove was virtually unknown in Britain up to the 1950's and since then it has spread across the country and increased in numbers. It first bred here in 1955. The bird spread at an average of 30 miles a year across the continent. Numbers increased by over 350% in the 40 years to 2012, but this growth has steadied now. At the same time the numbers of its near relative, the Turtle Dove, have declined dramatically. The same rapid spread of the Collared Dove has occurred in America as well, with the bird being found in most states of the country now. *Columba oenas* for the **Stock Dove** comes from the Latin columba for a pigeon or dove and the Greek oinas for a pigeon. *Streptopelia turtur* is the scientific name for the **Turtle Dove** which comes from the Greek streptos for collar and peleia a dove plus Latin turtur for the Turtle Dove. The **Woodpigeon**'s scientific name is *Columba palumbus* which comes from the Latin columba, a pigeon or dove and the Latin palumbes for woodpigeon.

Qi The **Common Crossbill**'s scientific name is *Loxia curvirostra* deriving from loxos meaning crosswise, curvus curved and rostrum beak. The Crossbill has the unusual ability of being able to to breed at any time of the year, with the breeding cycle being linked to the abundance of its preferred food crop, the spruce pine, not to a specific time of the year. The specialised bill enables the bird to extract the seeds from the newly formed cones, whereas other birds have to wait for the cones to mature and the seeds to fall out. The bird is transitory and can migrate considerable distances to find food. Mysteriously it is able to locate new sources of food many miles away. The **Scottish Crossbill**, *Loxia scotica* is now considered a separate species (i.e. it is not merely a sub-species of the Common Crossbill) and as such is the only bird (and indeed the only vertebrate) species that is endemic to Britain.

The **Common Scoter**'s scientific name is *Melanitta nigra* which comes from the Greek melas for black and netta, a duck plus the Latin niger for shining black.

A whole group of birds in the Finch family, Fringillidae, share the same scientific first name of *Carduelis* which is a word for the **Goldfinch** whose scientific name has two identical names *Carduelis carduelis*. The others are the **Common Redpoll**, *Carduelis flammea*, with *flammea*

107

referring to the birds red chin; the **Greenfinch**, *Carduelis chloris,* with *chloris* referring to the bird's green colour (chlorine being a green coloured gas); the **Lesser Redpoll**, *Carduelis cabaret,* with *cabaret* meaning entertainment (an unclear connection with the bird); the **Linnet**, *Carduelis cannabina, cannabina* being the Latin for hemp, a seed the bird eats; the **Serin**, *Serinus serinus* which comes from French serin for canary; the **Siskin**, *Carduelis spinus,* with *spinus* being a bird described by Aristophanes and finally the **Twite**, *Carduelis flavirostris* , with flavus meaning yellow and *rostris* bill. The Twite is the only British bird that comes from Tibet!

The **Coot**'s scientific name is *Fulica atra* which comes from the Latin fulica for coot and ater for black.

The **Crane**'s scientific name is simply *Grus grus* being the Latin for Crane.

Qi The **Cuckoo**'s scientific name is *Cuculus canorus* with *canorus* meaning melodious, as in a song. In 1381 Chaucer wrote "Summer is icumen in, lhude sing cucu" with the bird's name then being very similar to the Latin cuculus. The poem "In April he will come; in May he songs all day; in June he changes his tune; in July he prepares to fly; in August he must go" is quite accurate. In fact the males migrate earlier than August but he does change his tune during the season. In 2011 an interesting experiment was set up to plot the migration route of the bird. Six cuckoos were fitted with tracking devices and live data was sent plotting their outward and return routes (which differ). Centuries ago, when migration was a mystery, one belief was that from August until April Cuckoos turned into Sparrowhawks. Another belief was they hibernated in tree stumps.

Qi The obvious and most notable identification feature of the Curlew is its long, curved bill. Not surprisingly the scientific name is based on this, being *Numenius arquata* with *Numenius* from the Greek neos for new and mene for moon i.e. the crescent shaped new moon with the second word from the Latin arcuatus for bow-shaped. Its close relative the **Whimbrel** is named *Numenius phaeopus,* with *phaeopus* from the Greek phaios for dusky and pous for foot. The female Curlew is 20% heavier (at 850g) than the male and has a longer bill, which can reach down to food prey the male's bill cannot reach. Numbers in Britain have fallen by 62% over the last 40 years (to 2012).

The genus Calidris includes the **Sandpipers** with the word deriving from the Greek kalidris, which was used by Aristotle for a grey, waterside bird. This demonstrates how ancient the root of some bird's names are; the root of this name being 2 500 years old. The group includes the **Common Sandpiper**, *Actitis hypoleucos* which comes from aktites meaning coast dweller and hupo, below and leukos, white; **Curlew Sandpiper**, *Calidris ferruginea*, with ferrugo meaning rust, the colour of the breeding bird's breast; the **Dunlin**, *Calidris alpina*, with alpina from the Alps; the **Knot**, *Calidris canutus*, with canutus from a reference to King Canute (For detail see Page 158 'Some common folk lore'); **Little Stint**, *Calidris minuta*; **Purple Sandpiper**, *Calidris maritima* this bird is the most northerly breeding bird seen in Britain; and the **Sanderling**, *Calidris alba,* with *alba* meaning white.

The **Dunnock**'s scientific name is *Prunella modularis* which comes from the diminutive of the Latin prunus meaning brown plus modulari, to sing.

The **Eider** has already been mentioned as a bird with historical connections in this country going back to at least the 8th century. Both words in the scientific name *Somateria mollissima* refer to its down. The first word includes the Greek soma for body plus erion for wool and the second word *mollissima* very soft i.e. a very soft woolly body.

The **Fulmar**'s scientific name *Fulmarus glacialis* reflects the Old Norwegian for foul gull (from habits mentioned earlier) and *glacialis* from the Latin for its extreme northern range.

The **Gadwall** has the scientific name *Anas strepera* and is placed in the genus Anas, which simply means duck and strepera meaning noisy. In Muslim countries Anas is a boy's name indicating pleasantness, companionship and friendliness.

The **Garganey**'s name is *Anas querquedula*, with *querquedula* repetitively meaning duck. The Garganey is Britain's only summer visiting duck. Others in this genus with the first name of *Anas* are the **Mallard**, *Anas platyrhynchos*, with platus meaning broad and rhunkhos bill; the **Pintail**, *Anas acuta*, with *acuta* from the Latin acutus, sharp-pointed tail; the **Shoveler** *Anas clypeata*, with *clypeata* referring to shield-bearing bill; the **Teal**, *Anas crecca*, with *crecca* deriving from the Swedish name for the Teal, kricka and **Wigeon**, *Anas penelope* with the second word being the Greek penelops, a type of duck.

Qi The **Gannet**'s scientific name is *Morus bassanus*, with *Morus* from the Greek moros meaning silly, alluding to the ease with which the bird is caught, and *bassanus* after the Bass Rock in Scotland where the bird breeds in large numbers. The Gannet is expert at fishing, diving at up to 60 mph. Its nostrils are blocked off (it breathes through the side of its bill) to stop water flooding in, the base of its bill has a sponge-like damper and there are air sacs in the throat and breast to absorb the shock of hitting the water. The Gannet can dive to 20 m and fly long distances to feed. Unusually for a bird the female does not have a brood patch but uses its large webbed feet to provide warmth to the egg. The oldest living Gannet recorded was 37 years 4 months old.

The **Goldcrest**'s scientific name is *Regulus regulus* with *regulus* meaning little king, possibly referring to the bright orange head markings on the male bird. The **Firecrest**'s scientific name shares the genus name *Regulus* plus *ignicapilla* from the Latin igni for fire and capillus for cap, again referring to the male bird's bright head markings.

The **Golden Eagle** is an iconic bird and has been known for centuries, with many references to it in the Bible and other literature, appearances on ancient buildings, in art work, on national flags and coats of arms. Its scientific name is *Aquila chrysaetos* with *Aquila* being Latin for Eagle and *chrysaetos* the Greek khrusos for gold and aetos for Eagle. The bird appears in many mythical tales - see later section on myths. The bird appears in 'The dalliance of the Eagles' by Walt Witman 'Skyward in air a sudden muffled sound, the dalliance of eagles, the rushing amorous contact high in space together, The clinching interlocking claws, a living, fierce, gyrating wheel, Four beating wings, two beaks , a swirling mass grappling, In tumbling, turning clustering loops, straight downward fall.' The Golden Eagle has 1m cones in its eye compared to the 200 000 in a human eye. This would give the comparative size of a human eye the size of an orange. The bird also has two fovea on its retina, one to provide long distance focussing and the other for close distance focussing.

Qi Plover in the **Golden Plover**'s name is linked to the word plovere, to rain and the scientific name, *Pluvialis apricaria*, picks this up along with *apricaria*, from the Latin apricus meaning sun-kissed, a reference to the bird's golden summer plumage. The Golden Plover is part of the story of the instigation of the Guinness Book of Records. Whilst on a shooting party the Managing Director of Guinness had an argument over which was the fastest bird. Realising there was no suitable reference book available he founded the Guinness Book of Records in 1955, which is now the best selling copyrighted book ever. The **Grey Plover**'s scientific name is *Pluvialis squatarola* with *squatarola* an Italian name for a Plover.

Qi The **Goldeneye** is seen on estuaries in England during winter and has a distinctively shaped head, reflected in the scientific name *Bucephala clangula*. The first name derives from the Latin for bull and head (which seems about right!) and *clangula* from its loud double whistle. The duck is unusual in that it nests in holes in trees. The duck is also the target of partial brood parasitism, with other Goldeneyes, other ducks and even reports of Swallows laying their eggs in the Goldeneye's nest.

The **Goosander**'s names are almost identical, *Mergus merganser* with the ending anser, meaning Goose, being incorrect. The Goosander is a member of the Mergini family which include the saw tooths, referring to their serrated teeth used to catch their prey. The family includes the **Red-breasted Merganser** and the **Smew**. The scientific name of the Red-breasted Merganser, *Mergus serrator* describes the bird well with *serrator* meaning saw. The Smew's scientific name is *Mergellus albellus* with *albellus* meaning white, referring specifically to the male's high contrast black and white summer plumage.

Red-breasted Merganser

Qi The **Goshawk**'s scientific name is *Accipiter gentilis*, with *Accipiter* indicating Hawk from the verb meaning to grasp and *gentilis* for noble hawk. Like other Hawks the female, weighing 1,500 g, is heavier than the male at 850 g. The Goshawk is low down the falconer's hierarchy and was flown by a cook or poorman. A person who trains a Goshawk is called an austringer. The Goshawk appears on the flag of the Azores, with the name of islands deriving from the Portuguese for the bird - acor. In fact the Goshawk has never lived on the island, with the bird being confused with the Buzzard. Whilst the Goshawk is a relatively rare bird, its numbers have increased by over 400% over the last 25 years (according to the Rare Breeding Birds Panel report in 2014) to around 350 breeding pairs.

The **Grasshopper Warbler**'s distinctive song is reflected in its scientific name *Locustella naevia*, with *Locustella* meaning little locust or grasshopper and *naevia* spotted (plumage).

The **Great Grey Shrike**'s gruesome method of trapping its prey on spikes or thorns is reflected in its scientific name *Lanius excubitor*. *Lanius* is a butcher (hence the common name butcher bird) and *excubitor* for sentinel, as it sits and waits to single out its prey.

The **Great Northern Diver**'s scientific name, *Gavia immer*, comes from an old name for a sea-bird given by Pliny and the Icelandic for a surf roarer, based on the bird's ability to sit on the roughest of seas. The bird's close relatives, the **Black-throated Diver** has the scientific name *Gavia arctica* i.e. northern and the **Red-throated Diver** named *Gavia stellata*, with *stellata* meaning starry, possibly from the striking black and white pattern on the wing in summer plumage.

Great Spotted Woodpecker

Qi Not unsurprisingly the **Great Spotted Woodpecker**'s scientific name refers to its habit of drumming. The first word in *Dendrocopos major* comes from the Greek dendron for tree and kopos, cutter. To make the drumming sound the Woodpecker has to hit the tree trunk at just the right frequency (about 10 – 14 strikes per second) to set up a resonant frequency. The bird hits the tree with a force of about 1 kg and it has evolved a shock absorber at the base of the bill to prevent the drumming g forces causing serious brain damage. The brain is very solid and is unable to move around, plus the bone structure is modified to absorb the shock of drumming. The lower mandible also bends slightly to absorb the impact. In addition it has a nictitating membrane that covers its eyes as it strikes the tree to prevent debris injuring its eyes, plus feathers that cover the nostrils to prevent dust entering them. Both the male and female drum. Recent research has shown that Woodpeckers can identify the specific sounds made by individual birds. The Great Spotted Woodpecker's close relative the **Lesser Spotted Woodpecker** has the closely associated scientific name of *Dendrocopos minor*. Numbers of this bird have declined rapidly over the last 25 years (to 2012) by 82%. One reason is that its larger cousin has usurped its territories in woodland, particularly by taking over the Lesser Spotted Woodpecker's nests. The bird is hard to spot although it does drum like its bigger cousin, but is somewhat quieter and often remains hidden in the tree tops. The **Green Woodpecker**'s scientific name is *Picus viridis* which comes from the Greek pikos for a woodpecker and the Latin viridis, green.

The genus Tringa is another group of waders, with the word deriving from the Greek trungas, which was used by Aristotle for a waterbird. This group include the **Green Sandpiper**, *Tringa ochropus*, with *ochropus* meaning pale yellow foot; **Greenshank**, *Tringa nebularia*, with the second word mysteriously meaning possessing a mist; **Redshank**, *Tringa totanus*, with *totanus* being the Italian for the Redshank; **Spotted Redshank,** *Tringa erythropus*, with *erythropus* meaning simply red foot and finally the **Wood Sandpiper**, *Tringa glareola*, from glarea the Latin for gravel.

The **Grey Heron**'s scientific name is *Ardea cinerea* which comes from the Latin ardea for a heron and cinereus meaning ash-coloured (from cinis=ashes).

The **Grey Partridge**'s scientific name derives from a Greek mythological tale (recounted later) with the name Perdix perdix simply meaning a partridge. The **Red-legged Partridge**'s scientific name is

Alectoris rufa which comes from Greek alektoris for domestic hen and rufus, ruddy.

Qi The scientific name of the **Grey Phalarope** repeats the same meaning twice, the first word from the Greek and then the second from the Latin. The name *Phalaropus fulicarius* means coot-footed, which does not make a lot of sense as the bird is in the Sandpiper family Scolopacidae and has little in common with the Coot except that bird does have semi-lobed feet. The female Grey Phalarope is larger (at 63 g) than the male (50 g) and the birds demonstrate role reversal as the female is the brighter coloured bird, she chooses her mate and defends territory. The female arrives first at the breeding grounds and this behaviour is called protogny. Once she has laid her eggs she sets off on her migratory journey south, leaving the male to bring up the young. The male leaves the chicks before they can fly so, like many juveniles, they have to undertake their first migratory flight alone to some distant place.

A close relative of the Grey Phalarope is the **Red-necked Phalarope** whose scientific name is *Phalaropus lobatus* with *lobatus* meaning lobed. One bird tagged on Fetlar was found to have made a 16 000 km return migratory journey across the Atlantic, down to the Caribbean and thence to the Peruvian coast, and back again! All this by a bird weighing a mere 36 g and with a wing span of 36 cm. It is the only bird known to make this trip.

Surprisingly (given how small they are) Phalaropes are truly pelagic and increase their buoyancy on water by trapping air beneath their feathers.

The Wagtail family Motacillidae has three British family members. The **Grey Wagtail**'s scientific name is *Motacilla cinerea* which comes from the Greek muttex, a bird described by Hesychius and the Latin cinereus, ash-coloured, from cinis=ashes; the **Pied Wagtail** *Motacilla alba* with albus for white and the **Yellow Wagtail** *Motacilla flava* with flavus for yellow.

Qi The **Greylag Goose** has a boring and uninformative scientific name – *Anser anser*, merely meaning goose-goose! In a famous experiment Lorenz examined imprinting by these geese. At an early age goslings will attach themselves to whoever looks after them, including humans. Imprinting occurs at a specific phase when the birds are learning their behaviours for life. This learning does not require reward

116

or re-enforcement and is irreversible. Pliny recorded imprinting in the 1st century AD.

Qi The **Hawfinch** is an uncommon member of the Finch Fringilldae family and is a difficult bird to see as it spends much of its time in the tops of trees. It has a rather long scientific name which repeats the same information in both words i.e. *Coccothraustes coccothraustes* meaning to break a kernel. The bird is capable of cracking very hard nuts with its large beak and powerful muscles. Two horny pads on each of the upper and lower jaws help hold the nut in place and distribute the massive force evenly. The Hawfinch can create a pressure of 1000 times its own weight of 60 g, the equivalent of a human creating 60 tonnes of pressure.

The three British Harriers all share the same genus name of *Circus* based on the Greek for a hawk that flies in circles, being a distinctive feature of these birds. The scientific name of the **Hen Harrier** is *Circus cyaneus*, with *cyaneus* meaning dark blue; for the **Marsh Harrier**, *Circus aeruginosus*, from the Latin aerugo meaning copper and osus full, referring to the male's colouration and for the **Montagu's Harrier**, *Circus pygargus,* with *pygargus* coming from the Greek for a bird of prey mentioned by Aristotle.

Qi The **Hobby** is in the Falcon family, Falconidae and has the scientific name of *Falco subbuteo*, with *subbuteo* meaning smaller than a Buzzard, (which it is) *sub* meaning smaller and *buteo* being the scientific name for the **Buzzard**. *Falco* derives from the Latin falcis for sickle, referring to the bird's hooked talons. The name of the table football game came from the Hobby's scientific name! The creator of the game tried to register the name hobby, was not allowed to and so creatively improvised with the bird's Latin name. Other British birds in this family are the **Kestrel**, *Falco tinnunculus,* with *tinnunculus* meaning shrill sounding (from its call) and the **Merlin**, *Falco columbarius,* with the Latin columba meaning Pigeon, but the bird is too small to take a Pigeon. The **Peregrine** is the most widespread falcon in the world. Its scientific name is *Falco peregrinus* with *peregrinus* means wanderer, hence the word peregrination for journey or voyage. The latter word refers to the bird's migratory habit. Historically the bird was much valued and in the 17th century it was an offence to steal this bird. After the war numbers recovered only for the bird to be affected by DDT poisoning.

The **Honey-buzzard's** scientific name *Pernis apivorus* is more accurate than the English vernacular name. *Pernis* means a hawk, (the bird being closely related to the Kites which are in the Hawk family of Accipitridae) and *apivorus* means to devour a bee (or more correctly, it eats bee and wasp grubs); it doesn't eat honey. One estimate is that one irds will eat 90 000 grubs a year.

Qi The **House Martin's** scientific name is unusual in that it is an anagram; *Delichon urbicum* with *Delichon* being an anagram of the Greek khelidon (chelidon) for Swallow plus *urbicum* meaning city. The close connection with the Swallow is correct, as they are both Hirundines, members of the Hirundinidae family. Little is known about the wintering area of British House Martins, albeit it is somewhere in Africa. The use of geo locators fixed to the birds may well help solve this puzzle but these small birds still need to be caught after their migratory journey for the collected data to be down loaded. It is possible to fix heavier transmitters on larger birds, such as Cuckoos, and record the data live as the birds fly. Concerns have been raised about the recent fall in numbers (2014). The Hobby preys on House Martin, so the House Martin has developed a specific alarm call when it detects a Hobby. House Martin numbers have decreased by 45% over the last 40 years (Breeding Bird Survey in 2012).

Qi The close association of the **House Sparrow** to human habitation is reflected in the bird's scientific name *Passer domesticus*. Passeridae is the family name, with the **Tree Sparrow** having the same root plus *montanus* meaning mountain. In the 16th century boxes were erected near houses for the House Sparrow to nest in and when the birds bred the young were caught as a source of meat.

The scientific name of the **Jack Snipe** *Lymnocryptes minimus* reflects its behaviour and character, with *Lymnocryptes* from the Greek limne for marsh and krupto to hide. The bird is very difficult to see as it remains hidden until you are almost onto the bird, when it flies off quickly.

Qi The scientific name for the **Jay** (a member of the Crow family, Corvidae) is *Garrulus glandarius* which reflects key elements of the bird. *Garrulus* means to chatter (linked to the English word garrulous) and the bird can certainly be noisy, especially in autumn as it collects nuts for winter storage. *Glandarius* means producing acorns and the bird is highly adept at collecting and caching them. Jays can be seen anting in summer. They don't eat ants but use the ants to eliminate the parasites on their feathers by squeezing the ants to release formic acid which kills the parasites. The Jay is also a mimic and when it approaches carrion for a meal it makes a sound like a Buzzard to ward of intruders.

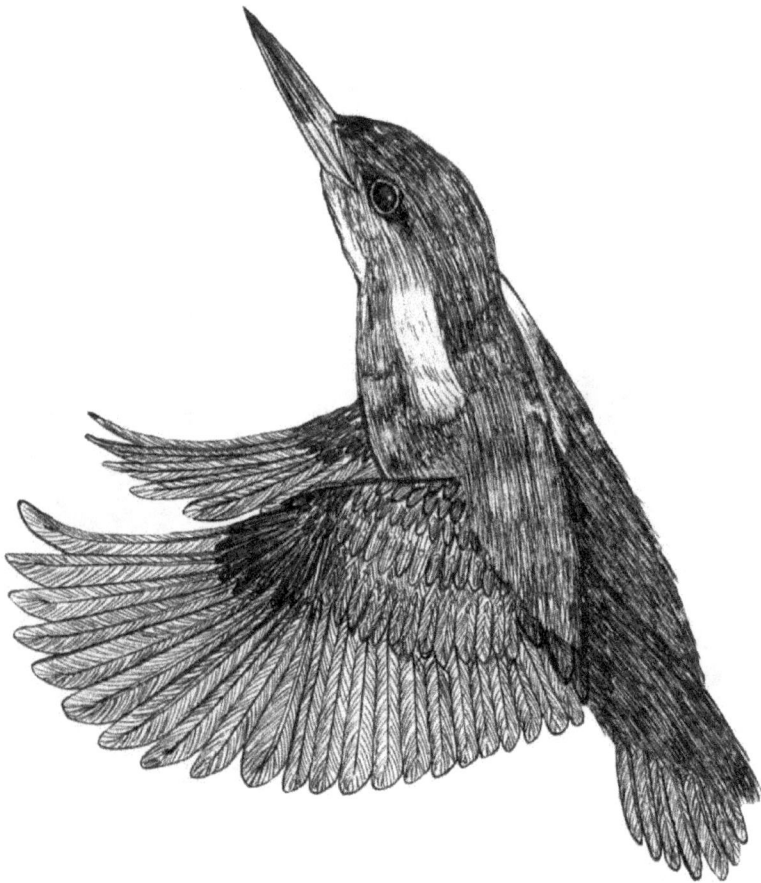

Qi The **Kingfisher** was a bird well known to the Greeks and appears in their mythology. Its scientific name, *Alcedo atthis*, references this connection, with *Alcedo* from the Greek alkuon for kingfisher. *Atthis* is name of one of Sappho's favourite young women from Lesbos. Sappho was a poet born in the 7th century BC who wrote about her love for Atthis.

The Kingfisher is a prodigious fisher and one pair were recorded taking 115 fish in one day. Over a good breeding season, with a pair having three broods, they can catch 8 000 fish! The bird can hover to locate its prey but more frequently sits on a branch and waits patiently. As the bird dives it closes its eyes, using a third, nictitating eyelid, and shuts its throat to stop water entering. The bird catches its fish prey by opening its mouth, rather than stabbing it. If the fish is for feeding to its young, or the male wants to present it to a potential female mate, it knows to turn the fish head to face out so the spines do not stick in the recipient's throat. The Kingfisher's nest is a chamber at the end of a tunnel between 60 and 90 cm long. The chamber is dark but the young have white tips on their bill to help the adults locate their bills for accurate feeding. The tunnel is excavated with about a 10 degree fall so that excrement drains out and away from the nest chamber to maintain hygiene. The bird's third and fourth toes are fused together to help dig their nest holes. A tell-tale sign of a nest site are the white droppings on the side of a sandy river bank. The Kingfisher also has a strategy of asynchronous hatching of its eggs (like birds of prey) i.e. the parents start to brood their eggs as soon as they are laid, with the first laid hatching first. This ensures that in times of food shortage the older, first laid siblings will survive and in times of plenty the whole brood will.

The Kingfisher's bright turquoise colouring of its feathers is produced by iridescence. The feathers have an intricate construction that causes interference of the light waves in such a way that the turquoise wavelength is produced. In very low light the feathers that appear turquoise in bright light are in fact brown. Birds' feathers' colouration is normally achieved by white light being absorbed by the feather's pigments, except for the wavelength of the colour we see.

The **Kittiwake**'s scientific name is *Rissa tridactyla* with *rissa* deriving from the Icelandic name rita and *tridactyla* meaning three-toed.

The **Lapwing**'s scientific name is *Vanellus vanellus* with vannus the Latin for a fan, referring to the bird's floppy flight.

The **Little Auk** is one of the most numerous birds in the world, estimated at 12m pairs. The bird's scientific name is an example of the name deriving from other languages, in this case Swedish. Its name is *Alle alle* which simply means a seabird (local to Oland). In Greenland birds are caught for food, being placed in a seal skin with seal fat and left to ferment.

Qi The **Little Egret**'s scientific name *Egretta garzetta* is based on a French and an Italian word. *Egretta* comes from the French aigrette, referring to the long, feathery neck plumes that were much used in millinery. *Garzetta* is Italian for little white heron (the bird is a member of the Heron family Ardeidae). In the 19th century the bird was shot for its prized plumes and there were protests to stop this practice. The movement to stop the killing of birds for their feathers eventually led to the formation of the Royal Society for the Protection of Birds (RSPB) in 1904. The first group, called The Plumage League, was set up in 1889 to 'discourage the wanton destruction of birds' and it became the Society for the Protection of Birds in 1891. Eventually legislation banned this trade. One London auction house alone in 1902 traded about 48 000 ounces of Heron feathers from an estimated 192 000 birds.

Qi The **Little Owl** is another bird which has been known since antiquity. Its scientific name is *Athene noctua* with *Athene* meaning wise from the connection to Athene, the Greek god of wisdom. *Noctua* was an Owl sacred to Minerva, a Roman goddess of wisdom. However, *noctua* means night and incorrectly associates this owl with the night as it is active during the day and twilight rather than night. The Little Owl was introduced to Britain from the Middle East in 1842 by a keen Northants ornithologist. It spread from there across the country. However recently numbers have declined, by 40% in the last 40 years (to 2011).

The **Little Ringed Plover** is in the family Charadriidae and has the scientific name *Charadrius dubius* from the Latin dubius from dubare meaning to vacillate. The **Ringed Plover** has the name *Charadrius hiaticula* which comes from the Greek kharadra, ravine and the Latin hiatus, a cleft and colere, to inhabit.

The **Long-eared Owl** and its close relative the Short-eared Owl share the same genus Asio, the name deriving from a horned owl, described by Pliny two millennia ago. The full scientific name for the Long-eared Owl is *Asio otus* with *otus* merely repeating another name for an eared owl and the **Short-eared Owl**'s name is *Asio flammeus* with *flammeus* referring to the fiery streaked plumage of the bird.

The **Long-tailed Duck** is in a genus all of its own – *Clangula*, which means to resound, from the male's yodelling call. Its full name is *Clangula hyemalis* with *hyemalis* meaning wintry. The duck is the deepest diving sea duck reaching depths of 60m.

The **Magpie's** scientific name is simply *Pica pica*, a general name for pied birds, with pied formerly meaning coloured.

A trick quiz question is 'which bird has the scientific name *Puffinus puffinus*?'. Many fall for the obvious answer, **Puffin**, which is of course wrong. As explained earlier on in the Section 'Individual bird names', for a long time there was confusion in naming the **Manx Shearwater** and the Puffin, with the former acquiring the scientific name *Puffinus puffinus*. The Puffin's scientific name is *Fratercula arctica* with *Frater* meaning friar or brother and *cula* small, referring to the bird's head feather pattern and *arctica* meaning northern. An alternative meaning of *Fratercula* is a reference to the way the bird holds its feet in flight as though at prayer.

Qi The **Marsh Warbler's** scientific name is *Acrocephalus palustris*, with *Acrocephalus* from the Greek akros pointed and kephale head, and palus meaning marsh. This bird is a master mimic of other birds' songs, incorporating up to 76 other birds' songs. The song of the Marsh Warbler in Britain was analysed and the results perplexed the scientists, as they could only identify about half of the songs mimicked but not the others. The mystery was solved when a researcher went to the bird's Kenyan winter quarters and discovered that the other songs being mimicked were Kenyan bird songs! The bird is a rare breeder in Britain with only about 30 breeding pairs.

Two other birds sharing the same genus name of *Acrocephalus* with the Marsh Warbler are the **Reed Warbler** and the **Sedge Warbler**. Their respective scientific names are *Acrocephalus scirpaceus* with scirpus meaning reed (where the bird breeds) and *Acrocephalus schoenobaenus* from the Greek skhoiniklos for reed and baino to walk. Indeed, the Sedge Warbler can sometimes be seen straddling near the top of reeds whilst singing its distinctive song.

The **Meadow Pipit** is part of the genus *Anthus* which includes the Rock Pipit, Tree Pipit and Water Pipit with *Anthus* coming from the Greek for a small grassland bird named by Aristotle. The Meadow Pipit's scientific name is *Anthus pratensis* with *pratensis* meaning found in meadows. Logic persists and the **Rock Pipit**'s scientific name is *Anthus petrosus* with *petrosus* meaning rock. The **Tree Pipit**'s is *Anthus trivialis* with *trivialis* meaning common as in ordinary (the bird is not common in Britain where numbers have fallen by 77% in the last 40 years) and the **Water Pipit**'s name is *Anthus spinoletta* with *spinoletta* the Italian for a little lark.

The **Moorhen**'s scientific name is an apt description of the bird, being *Gallinula chloropus* with *Gallinula* being Latin for a little hen, a diminutive of gallina (meaning hen). *Chloropus* is comprised of the Greek khloros for green (as in the green coloured gas, chlorine) and pous for foot i.e. a green footed hen; spot on! The family name commonly used for the Moorhen and its relatives is gallinule. The North American name for this bird is Common Gallinule.

The Moorhen exhibits partial brood parasitic behaviour, where sometimes females lay a few of their own eggs in another couple's nest to boost their breeding success. If timed right, the host parents will incubate the egg and feed the fledgling as the host often does not recognise the addition of an extra egg. The Cuckoo is well known for this behaviour but it is the only British bird which is wholly brood parasitic. Along with the Moorhen, several other birds are partially brood parasitic.

Qi The **Nightingale** is a well-known songster but regrettably numbers have fallen dramatically. A BTO survey reported a 91% drop in numbers over the 40 years to 2007. More recently the Breeding Bird

Survey reported a fall of 43% over the 17 years to 2012 with an estimated 3,300 territories held but with a distinct shift towards the

bird breeding only in the South East of England. The bird's scientific name is *Luscinia megarhynchos* which is a curious name. *Luscinia* comes from the Latin luctus for lament and cano to sing, i.e. singing a lamentation. Most listeners would not call the bird's complex, powerful and varied song a lament. Many would agree with Izak Walton who wrote "it breathes such sweet music out of her little instrumental throat that it might make mankind think miracles had not ceased". Note the historical common error in thinking that it is the female which sings. Boris Pasternak writing in Doctor Zhivago makes the case for the bird's song being unique "Once again I wondered at the difference between their (Nightingale's) song and that of all other birds, at the wide gulf left unabridged by nature between the others and the wealth and singularity of theirs. Such variety and power and resonance".

Several poets have written about the bird's distinctive song. For example, John Milton in 'Nightingale' wrote 'O nightingale, that on yon bloomy spray Warbl'st at eve, when all the woods are still, Thou with fresh hope the lover's heart doth fill, While the jolly hours lead on propitious May; Thy liquid notes that close the eye of the day, First heard before the shallow cuckoo's bill, portend success in love.' and John Keats in 'Ode to a Nightingale' - My heart aches, and a drowsy numbness pains My sense, as though of hemlock I had drunk, Or emptied some dull opiate to the drains 'Tis not through envy of thy happy lot, But being too happy in thine happiness - That thou, light-winged Dryad of the trees, In some melodious plot Of beechen green, and shadows number less, Singest of summer in full-throated ease.

An explanation for the reference to lament in the name can be found in Greek mythology as part of the story of Philomena. This is recounted in the Section 'Some common myths and stories'. *Megarhynchos* means large bill. Again, the bird has a slim bill as expected for an insectivore. It is the male bird that sings, despite early literature stating it was the female (but the sexes are identical). The Nightingale does sing at night and also during the day. Its song is complex and analysis has discovered 250 phrases. Its song is also very loud – up to 90 dBA and the bird will sing louder to counter-act any background noise. The male sings up to the time when its mate lays her eggs and then it stops singing; unless the brood is lost and then it will start to sing again. It is highly unlikely that the 'Nightingale sang in Berkeley Square' as this area would never have provided the right environment for the bird; it was probably a Robin singing, which is a close relative of the Nightingale in the Turdidae family.

Qi Another bird with a fascinating mythological story behind its name is the **Nightjar**. Its scientific name is *Caprimulgus europaeus*. This is

recounted in the section 'Some common folk lore'. The bird was known to Aristotle and is mentioned in the Bible as a night hawk, which states that the bird should not be eaten as it is unclean. The Nightjar is a summer migrant to Britain and is found on open heath land. It is predominantly nocturnal but can be seen at sunset as it starts its night time moth hunting activity. Otherwise it is difficult to spot as its colouration blends so well into its surroundings including when it's sitting on a bare tree branch or when the female is sitting fully camouflaged on its ground nest.

The Nightjar is adapted to detecting moths on the wing through a set of sensitive rictal bristles around its mouth. The prey is caught using the serrations on their toes and transferred to their mouth. These serrations are used to keep the bristles clean. The male's song is a rapid chirring noise emitting up to 1900 notes per minute and seemingly singing continuously without breathing!

The **Osprey**'s scientific name is *Pandion haliaetus* with *Pandion* referring to a mythical Greek king Pandion and *haliaetus* deriving from the Greek halos for sea and aetos for Eagle. The Osprey is in the family Pandionidae and Eagles in the family Accipitridae but they are in the same order of Falconiformes.

The **Oystercatcher**'s scientific name is accurately descriptive: *Haematopus ostralegus* which translates as the blood-footed oyster catcher.

The **Pheasant**'s scientific name is *Phasianus colchicus* with *Phasi* referring to the river Phasis in modern day Western Georgia, where

Pheasants were reportedly found and Colchis a city in Georgia. The bird was introduced into Britain by the Normans in the 11th century and possibly earlier by the Romans.

The **Pied Flycatcher**'s scientific name is *Ficedula hypoleuca* with

Ficedula meaning fig eating perhaps referring to their diet of fruit and seeds whilst migrating, and *hypoeuca* the Greek hupo for below and leukos for white.

The **Pink-footed Goose**'s scientific name is *Anser brachyrhynchus* which comes from the Latin *anser* for goose and the Greek brakhus for short and rhunkhos for bill.

Qi The **Ptarmigan**'s scientific name is *Lagopus muta* with *Lagopus* deriving from lago for hare and pus for foot. The bird has feathered feet and toes resembling a hare. This affords its feet protection from the cold as it lives at high altitudes all year round and seldom comes below 600 m. The bird unusually has feathers on its eye lids to protect against the cold. Muta means silent but the bird croaks so it is not as silent as implied by the name. This also contradicts the formal English name as this derives from the Gaelic for croaker.

The **Quail**'s scientific name is another repetitive name, *Coturnix coturnix* which comes from Latin coturnix for quail.

Razorbill

The **Razorbill**'s scientific name shows how the Latin name can be a Latinised version of words from a different language i.e. *Alca torda* with *Alca* coming from Old Norsk and *torda* from Icelandic, both being names for the Razorbill.

Qi The **Red Grouse** also has a similar scientific name to the Ptarmigan - *Lagopus lagopus*. The Red Grouse is famous for the shoots which start on the 'glorious twelfth' of August, established by the Game Act in 1773, and finish on the 10th December. Gamekeepers were highly vigilant at preserving their stocks and shot any birds that might kill their precious game birds. A few still do, although it is illegal. One record of the extent of a gamekeeper's predator control is seen in the killing in 3 years of 98 Peregrines, 78 Merlin, 462 Kestrels, 475 Ravens, 3 Honey-buzzards, 15 Golden Eagles, 27 White-tailed Eagles, 18 Osprey, 63 Goshawks, 275 Red Kites, 68 Harriers and 109 Owls on one estate! Regrettably the practice of killing wild birds of prey to protect game birds is still prevalent in some areas. An RSPB report published in 2015 gave an accurate, central record of crimes relating to the killing of wild birds over a 20-year time period. This confirmed the illegal killing of 779 protected birds of prey and represents only the reported and detected crimes whereas many more may well have been killed but remained undetected.

The **Red Kite**'s scientific name is *Milvus milvus* simply from the Latin milvus a kite.

The **Ring-necked Parakeet** has in recent times become a common bird in SE England, to the extent that for some it is now a pest, as it usurps the nest holes of other birds and its roosts are very noisy. It is Britain's only naturalised Parrot having established itself in the wild in 1969, probably from escapees. The scientific name is *Psittacula krameri* with *Psittacula* being a diminutive of psittacus for parrot and *krameri* after the 18th century scientist W H Kramer.

The **Robin**'s scientific name is *Erithacus rubecula* which comes from Greek erithakos for robin and Latin ruber for red.

Qi The **Rock Dove**'s scientific name is associated with the Romans, who bred the birds in dovecotes called columbariums. Hence the name *Columba livia* with *livia* shortened from the female name Olivia which means life. Possibly the name is connected to the olive branch which signified to Noah the return of life on earth after the biblical flood.

Qi The **Ruddy Duck**'s scientific name is *Oxyura jamaicensis* with *Oxyura* coming from the Greek for sharp-tailed, as it is, being a member of the so-called stiff-tails, and then Jamaica, which refers to Jamaica Bay in North America where it was observed breeding. The bird is very aggressive and on the continent it hybridised (cross bred) with the White-headed Duck until the latter was almost extinct. This led to a vigorous debate about culling the Ruddy Duck. Some argued that nature should be allowed to take its course, others that an introduced bird that is having a detrimental effect on another species should be controlled. In the event a cull was carried out and numbers of the bird in Britain are now very low, with some escapes from wildfowl collections.

Qi The scientific name of the **Ruff** is *Philomachus pugnax* with both words referring to the male bird's fighting spirit expressed in the vigorous lek displays used to attract a female. *Philomachus* is Greek for pugnacious and *pugnax* the Latin for fight. Numbers of this bird are precariously low and in the early 1990's only five females bred in the UK.

The **Sand Martin**'s scientific name is simply *Riparia riparia* with ripa meaning bank. The bird is in the Hirundinidae family, along with the House Martin and the Swallow. All three are summer migrants to Britain. The idea of birds migrating took a long time to establish and tales to explain where the birds went in winter abounded. Whilst they are fanciful now at the time they were taken seriously. A common explanation for the Hirundines not being seen in winter was that they hibernated at the bottom of pools. This was partly based on the fact that flocks of these birds were seen near reed beds as they congregated and fed before disappearing - into the mud, as the tale has it. Now we know they congregate in reed beds before they migrate south. In the 16th century fishermen attested that they were able to pull the birds out of the mud and revive them by holding them in front of a fire! This was given official credence by a Royal Society investigation in the 1660's. It took until the 19th century for migration to become an established and universally accepted fact.

The **Scaup**'s scientific name is *Aythya marila* which comes from the Greek aithuia for a seabird described by Aristotle and the Greek marile for charcoal embers.

Shag

Qi The **Shag** was known to Aristotle and its scientific name means Aristotle's cormorant, with the names Shag and Cormorant often used interchangeably. The name is *Phalacrocorax aristotelis* with *Phalacrocorax* being made up of phalakros meaning bald and korax Raven, which seems odd as both the male and female Shag both have a prominent tuft on their heads when in breeding plumage! Indeed, this is where its English name Shag comes from. The Shag is a deep sea diver reaching depths of 45 m, predominantly feeding on the sea bottom. The **Cormorant**'s scientific name is *Phalacrocorax carbo* with *carbo* meaning black, as in charcoal. Britain holds about 40% of the world population of Shag. Like Cormorants, Shag have poor water-proofing on their feathers. This improves their ability to swim under water but they then have to dry their feathers by spreading out their wings. Because of this they only migrate short distances. Birds are very faithful to their wintering quarters with some birds returning to the same spot on a harbour wall! Shag were shot during World War 2 for restaurant food.

The **Shelduck**'s scientific name *Tadorna tadorna* comes from the French tadorne for Shelduck.

The **Shore Lark** is a winter bird in Britain found on shores, hence the English name. The scientific name is *Eremophila alpestris*. The first word derives from the Greek eremos meaning desert and philos for loving. The bird is found on open land and pararies in America. *Alpestris* is Latin for the Alps or mountains where the bird breeds. A strange geographical mixture!

The **Skylark**'s scientific name is *Alauda arvensis* with *Alauda* meaning Lark and *arvensis* of a field, being a simple, accurate description.

The **Snipe**'s scientific name is *Gallinago gallinago* which simply means hen-hen.

Qi The **Snow Bunting** has now been placed in a different family (Calcariidae) from the Buntings (Emberizidae) as the result of DNA analysis. So the formal English name is now incorrect, placing it in the wrong family. The bird's scientific name is *Plectrophenax nivalis*. *Plectrophenax* derives from the Greek plektron for cock's spur and *phenax* meaning impostor. The Greek word is accurate as the bird is now placed in the family whose common name is long-spurs. The Snow Bunting has a long hind toe nail to assist in walking. *Nivalis* is from the Latin nivus for snow. The bird also has feathered legs to protect it from the severe cold environment it lives in during its breeding season. The male bird returns first to the breeding area where temperatures can be as low as -30 °C. It is one of only three birds to have been sighted at the North Pole. It is the most northerly breeding bird in the world along with the Raven. As there are very few natural predators the bird has a very high (75%) fledgling success rate. Unusually the Snow Bunting only moults once a year, possibly to minimise the energy drain of moulting twice.

The **Sparrowhawk**'s scientific name is *Accipter nisus* with *Accipter* from the Latin accipere meaning to grasp and *nisus* another name for the Sparrowhawk. *Nisus* dervies from the myth of Nisus, King of Megara, who was turned into a bird of prey after the city was betrayed by his daughter Scylla, who was turned into a lark, forever flying in fear of her father.

The **Spotted Flycatcher**'s scientific name of *Muscicapa striata* reflects the bird's habits. Musca is Latin for fly and capere to seize and *striata* from stria meaning line. Numbers of this bird have declined by 87% in the 40 years to 2010.

Qi The **Starling**'s scientific name is *Sturnus vulgaris* with *Sturnus* meaning starling and *vulgaris* common (not rude or vulgar!). The Starling is a great mimic. Birds acquire new sounds and a larger repertoire makes them more attractive to prospective mates. Mozart kept a Starling as a pet and it is believed the musical joke pieces he wrote were inspired by the bird. The Starling is one of the few British birds to practice partial brood parasitism, whereby a female will lay her eggs in the nest of another Starling if she cannot find a nest of her own. The Cuckoo is the only British bird that practices full brood parasitism.

The **Stonechat**'s scientific name is *Saxicola torquatus* which derives from the Latin saxum for rock and colere to dwell i.e. a rock dweller plus the Latin torquis for collar.

The **Stone-curlew**'s scientific name continues the unusual-name theme for this bird! The name is *Burhinus oedicnemus*. *Burhinus* is comprised of the Greek bous for bull and rhinos for nose plus oideo for swelling and kneme for knee. So the bird's name becomes bull-nosed swollen knee! The bird has a comparatively short, slim bill and does not resemble a bull! As noted earlier, the 'knee' is in fact a swollen ankle. So none of the names for this bird are wholly accurate!

The **Storm Petrel**'s scientific name accurately describes the bird - *Hydrobates pelagicus*. This derives from the Greek hudro for water and baino to tread and pelagos for the open sea. A water-treading bird of the open sea is exactly right!

The **Swallow**'s scientific name is *Hirundo rustica*, simply *Hirundo* for the swallow and *rustica* for rural. The Swallow's nesting habits mean that in Britain closely associate it with human habitation rather than the open countryside.

It was noted earlier that the **Swift** has small, weak feet and this is stated twice in its scientific name of *Apus apus* i.e. foot-less, foot-less. The Swift is the only British bird in the order Apodiformes, genetically a long way from the Swallow to which it is often connected.

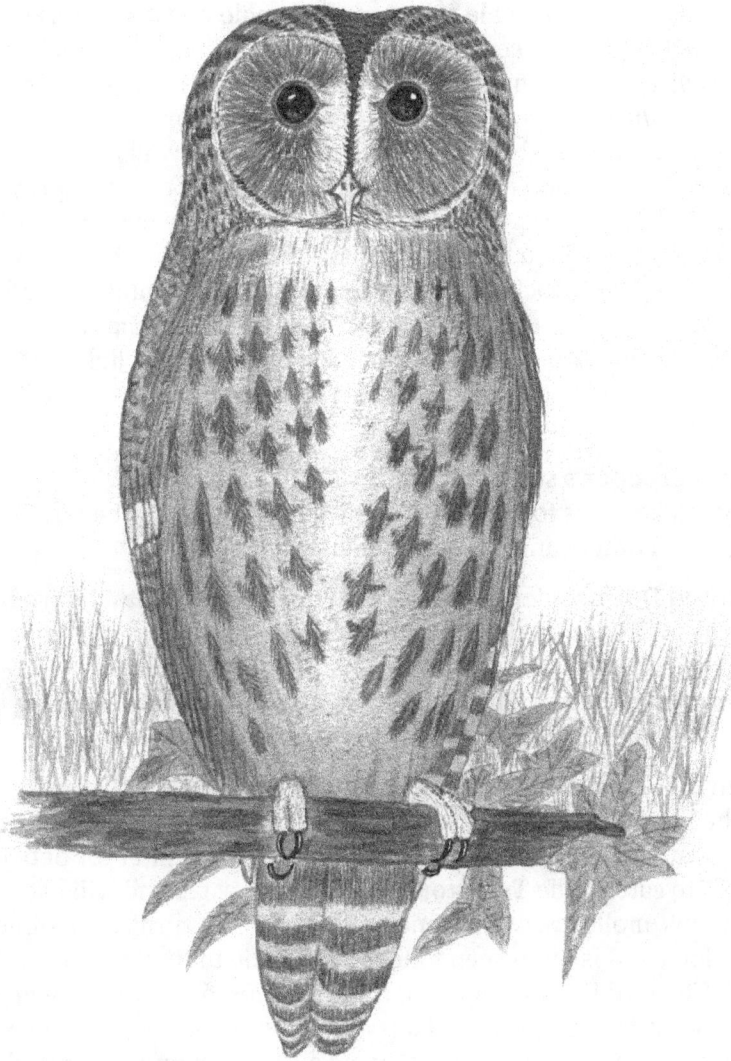

Qi The **Tawny Owl** being nocturnal is heard much more often than it is seen, with the hu...huoooo hoot and a u-wee sound being familiar woodland, night-time sounds. Often these two sounds are put together as tu-whit, to-woo but the hoot is made by the male and the other sound is the female's response. The Tawny Owl is one of the few British birds who sing a duet i.e. the male calls and the female responds. It is thought that this behaviour is a co-operative defence against intruders. The Tawny Owl's scientific name is *Strix aluco* with *Strix* being the Greek for an Owl and *aluco* deriving from the Italian allocco for Tawny Owl. Being a nocturnal hunter the bird has very large eyes and whilst it has reasonable night vision it uses its enhanced hearing to locate prey, as explained earlier in respect of the Barn Owl. Its large eyes have a 13 mm pupil (compared to 8 mm in humans) and as result the Owl cannot rotate its eyes in its socket and has to move its head round instead. Also the Owl sees in black and white rather than colour as it has a higher proportion of photoreceptor rods on its retina to collect light (as opposed to cones that detect colour) as rods are more light sensitive than cones.

The **Tree Creeper**'s scientific name is *Certhia familiaris* which comes from Greek kerthios for a small tree-dwelling bird described by Aristotle and others and the Latin familiaris-familiar.

The **Tufted Duck**'s scientific name is *Aythya fuligula* with *Aythya* being the Greek for a seabird described by Aristotle and *fuligula* from the Latin fuligo for soot and gula for throat. The Tufted Duck is comparatively recent arrival to Britain, first recorded as breeding in 1849.

The **Turnstone**'s scientific name is *Arenaria interpres* with *Arenaria* from the Latin arena for sand, but the bird is associated with stony beaches rather than sand. *Interpres* is comprised of inter for between and pres to catch. The Turnstone has catholic tastes and will eat crustaceans, molluscs, worms and even carrion. It turns over stones to release food and is often seen following the tide to find its food under stones. The bird is strong enough to turn stones over weighing nearly its own body weight. Each bird has a slight variation in plumage which enables the birds to identify those in its own group and any intruders from another group.

The **Water Rail**'s scientific name is *Rallus aquaticus* with *Rallus* the Latin for rail, referring to the bird's voice and *aquaticus* to its watery environment.

The **Waxwing**'s scientific name is *Bombycilla garrulus* with *Bombycilla* from the Greek bombukos for silk and cilla for tail, reflecting the very smooth appearance of the bird's feathers. *Garrulus* means chattering, which the bird does. The Waxwing is a winter visitor to Britain and is seen in large numbers some years when the rowan berry crop of its native Scandinavia is poor, causing migratory irruptions. The bird has a voracious appetite and one bird was observed eating 500 berries in 6 hours, about 3 times its own weight!

The **Wheatear** has a repetitive scientific name - *Oenanthe oenanthe* deriving from the Greek oenos for wine and anthos for flower, based on the time of the bird's return from its winter quarters, being when the vines flower in Greece.

The **Whinchat**'s scientific name is *Saxicola rubetra* which comes from the Latin saxum for rock and colere to dwell plus Latin rubetra, a type of small bird.

The **White-fronted Goose** is named *Anser albifrons*, *Anser* for goose and albus white and frons brow, reflecting the key identification feature of this Goose.

Qi The **White-tailed Eagle** is the largest bird of prey in Britain and the fourth largest Eagle in the world and has the largest wing span of any British bird at 2.2 m. By 1918 the bird had been driven to extinction, being killed for its predatory behaviour. Attempts were made to re-introduce the birds in 1975, using birds from Norway. It took until 1985 for successful breeding to occur on Mull. This population has grown and further introductions have been made in western Scotland, with 65 territories established by 2012. The White-tailed Eagle's scientific name is accurate, being *Haliaeetus albicilla*. This is comprised of halos for sea, aetos for Eagle, albus for white and cilla for tail - a white-tailed sea eagle. Fishermen had a tale that as soon as fish saw the bird they rose to the surface, belly up, to be caught. That led to fishermen using Eagle fat on their bait to tempt fish to bite!

The **Woodcock**'s scientific name is *Scolopax rusticola* which comes from the Greek skolopax for the woodcock and the Latin rusticus for rural and colere to dwell.

The **Woodlark**'s scientific name is *Lullula arborea* with *Lullula* based on lula as onomatopoeic and *arborea* meaning of trees. The bird's habitat is heath land with few trees rather than woodland. The Lark uses trees as a perch from which to launch it aerial song flight.

The

Qi The **Wren**'s scientific name is *Troglodytes troglodytes*, meaning cave-dweller, is based on a tale recounted later the Section 'Some common folk lore'. The Wren has established a colony on Shetland, the Outer Hebrides and St Kilda. These birds have gradually evolved physically and now differ from the mainland Wren. They are paler, have a longer, thicker bill (perhaps arising from dietary change) and a different song. In winter our population is supplemented by birds that migrate from Russia to Britain. In another marvel of migration a bird weighing 10g flies non-stop over the North Sea often in poor weather! The birds roost in numbers in cold weather, with one recorded roost of 63 birds in one nest! Number have increased in Britain by 100% in the last 40 years.

Qi The **Wryneck**'s scientific name is *Jynx torquilla* from the Greek iunx for Wryneck and *torquilla* from the Latin torquere meaning to twist. The word *Jynx* derives from a Roman myth that if you bind a Wryneck to spinning wheel (called an iynx) this would lure a potential partner or sweetheart. This member of the Woodpecker family has a comparatively shorter bill and whilst it has feet with two toes pointing forwards and two backwards, it lacks the stiff tail feathers of its cousins so it cannot feed by clinging to the side of a tree and has to find its food on the ground. Small numbers of Wryneck pass through Britain in spring and autumn as they migrate but the bird no longer breeds in Britain. In 1909 the bird was described as 'plentiful'.

COLLECTIVE NOUNS

Why birds flock

One key aspect of bird behaviour that humans have observed and been fascinated by is when birds flock. Some birds are highly gregarious and flock in huge numbers. The Starling is a bird notable for the size of its roost flocks. Large numbers gather at dusk to settle in trees and bushes to feel secure. Waders are a group of birds that often gather in huge flocks. As they feed on the vast open spaces of estuaries they are vulnerable to predation, so they flock to minimise this risk. One of the most spectacular bird-watching sights is to see a huge flock of Knot take to the air and swirl round, making fantastic shapes as they wheel up, round and down. The birds seem to work in unison and never seem to collide with each other. It is thought that light coloured wing bars assist in following neighbours. One scientist worked out that any one bird needs to be able to keep check on the position of their nearest seven neighbours in order to avert collisions. Of course, many other species of animal, insect and fish all display this behaviour e.g. herds of animals, swarms of insects and shoals of fish.

Birds gather together in large groups for a number of reasons. One is security. Smaller birds are always on the alert for a predatory bird looking for a tasty meal. A flock confuses the potential predator who finds it difficult to pick off one from amongst a swirling mass of birds. Within flocks of Thrush and other ground feeding birds, individuals take it in turns to look up for potential danger and then alert the whole group. This means that the majority of birds can concentrate on eating. When alerted they all fly off in a flock to comparative safety e.g. to a nearby tree. Other birds will collectively mob a predator. When Blackbirds detect a Tawny Owl in a wood they attack it with great noise and ferocity until the Owl is forced to fly off.

For similar reasons of security some birds nest colonially. A common example of this are Rooks who form large rookeries in tall trees. By nesting together their young are more secure against predators. Again individuals alert the group to a threat and will collectively attack a marauding predator.

During severe cold weather birds flock to stay warm. For example, Wrens will gather together to keep warm and Pied Wagtails gather in large flocks, often in trees in town centres. Herons are very much solitary birds but they can sometimes be seen standing huddled together in cold weather to keep warm.

In a few species of birds, males gather in groups to attract a mate. This behaviour has been noted for Black Grouse, Red Grouse and Ruff. Black Grouse gather in leks during autumn, when no females are present, possibly to establish territory. All these birds gather in leks in spring to attract a female and mate. By utilising this behaviour the males are making themselves visible to a greater number of females thus increasing their chances of successfully mating.

Geese and Swans (amongst other birds) undertake their migratory flights in family flocks. Typically they fly in a V formation which is aerodynamically efficient. The Swan or Goose at the front (often an adult bird) has to use the most energy with the birds behind benefitting from the vortices of air produced by the lead bird. Periodically the birds shift position and another bird will take over the energy-sapping lead duties for a time. This group behaviour also ensures that the juveniles are guided to the feeding ground or roost destination and can learn from the adults. The V formation also enhances communication and coordination within the group.

Some birds flock to find food. A shoal of mackerel will quickly attract the attention of a flock of Gannets. In winter members of the Tit family will form flocks to forage for food, which can often be scarce then.

It is not unusual for birds to form mixed flocks. High tide roosts on estuaries are often comprised of several species, often presenting birdwatchers with an interesting identification challenge. Lapwings traditionally mix with Golden Plovers in fields left fallow for the winter.

As with any set of behaviours there are advantages and disadvantages and birds will obviously choose the behaviour that on balance improves their chance of survival and successful breeding. The disadvantages of flocking include the greater risk of spreading disease. When a large number of birds flock together in close proximity, any diseased bird can infect its neighbour.

Birds that flock also present a greater visible presence to a potential predator. Whilst the overall chance of an individual bird being caught is lower, predators can see a flock easily. Often a predator will look for a weak individual to pick off. A Peregrine hunting a flock of small ducks or waders will look for a weaker bird that cannot stay within the close confines of the flock. The bird of prey can then catch this individual with comparative ease.

Humans, having been aware of birds gathering together for the reasons outlined above, have given names to these flocks which we call collective nouns. Some birds, which habitually flock, have been given several collective nouns. Below is a list of collective nouns, in alphabetical order of the bird's formal English name. For ease, some birds (often from the same family) which share the same collective noun appear together.

List of collective nouns

The **Barn Owl** - parliament; stare; study and wisdom. Parliament as a collective noun is shared with the **Carrion Crow** and **Rook** as well as the other Owls. Predictably the names reflect the characteristic of wisdom that some cultures have ascribed to Owls. The **Little Owl**, **Long-eared Owl**, **Short-eared Owl** and the **Tawny Owl** all share the same collective nouns.

Geese are often seen in flocks on the ground in winter as they graze in fields and also as they fly from feeding ground to roost. Collective nouns for the **Barnacle Goose** include gaggle; nide; plump; skein and wedge. Gaggle refers to a group on the ground. It is also used more generally to describe a disorderly group of people. A plump refers to when they are flying closely together and skein refers to the birds in flight and wedge to the characteristic shape of their flight pattern. These collective nouns also apply to the **Bean Goose, Brent Goose, Canada Goose, Greylag Goose, White-fronted Goose** and the **Pink-footed Goose**.

Wedge is also used to describe a flock of **Swans**, who also fly in a V formation. This applies to **Bewick's Swan** and the **Whooper Swan**, both of whom are winter visitors to Britain. They fly considerable distances on migration in family groupings, similar to geese. The Bewick's Swan breeds on the Arctic tundra and the Whooper Swan further east.

Collective nouns for the **Bittern** include sedge and siege. These nouns are also apply to flocks of **Grey Heron**. Neither bird is gregarious but will flock in extreme weather conditions.

The **Black-headed Gull** forms noisy, energetic flocks and the collective nouns reflect this, such as colony; leash; pack; screech and squabble. They form mixed flocks with other birds as they seek to chase them to pinch their food.

Flocks of **Bar-tailed Godwit** are interestingly called a omniscience; pantheon and prayer. Why this bird is referred to as all knowing is not clear. Pantheon derives from the Greek pantheion with pan meaning all and theion holy. It could be that the collective noun prayer comes from the fact that the god in Godwit means good (to eat).

The **Black Grouse's** unusual courtship ritual has already been noted, when many males gather at a traditional lek. Other collective nouns include brood (shared with the Red Grouse); covey, a common collective noun for game birds and pack.

The **Bullfinch** is most often seen in pairs rather than in a flock. However, if they group together they are called a bellowing. Again this is strange as the Bullfinch is a quiet bird and is not given to bellowing! It can sing very well when trained.

A flock of **Buzzard** is called a wake.

The collective noun for a group of **Capercaillie** is tok.

The **Chaffinch** frequently form flocks and names for this include charm; trembling and trimming. It shares these nouns with the **Goldfinch**. The word charm derives from the Latin carmen meaning magical song.

The **Chough** has two collective nouns, chattering and clattering. The former noun is also used for some Finches.

Collective nouns for the **Collared Dove** include kit and loft.

A flock of **Common Sandpiper** is called a fling.

One collective noun for the **Common Tern** is dread.

The **Coot** is seen in loose groups on open water in winter. These have been described as a commotion, from its petulant, belligerent behaviour; cover; fleet; pod; raft, a collective noun used for many ducks; rasp and swarm.

Cormorant are colonial nesters and collectively they are called a gulp or flight.

Curlew congregate in large flocks in winter on estuaries and have the collective nouns of head and herd.

The **Dotterel's** collective noun is a trip as is the **Dunlin's.**

Ducks as general group have a range of collective nouns ascribed to them including badelyne; brace, usually a dead pair; doping, when diving; flush; paddling; plump; raft, when on water; safe; skein; sord; stream; team and twack.

The **Gadwall**, being a duck shares the collective nouns of balding; paddling; raft and sord with **Pintail, Pochard, Teal, Tufted Duck** and **Wigeon**.

142

Collective nouns for the **Golden Eagle** include congregation, which it shares with the **Golden** and **Grey Plover**; congress; convocation and jubilee.

The **Golden Plover** gathers in large flocks in winter, often with **Lapwing**. Collective nouns include band; congregation; knob, whilst on water; a rush in flight; stand and wing.

The **Goldfinch** shares the nouns charm; trembling and trimming with the **Chaffinch** plus the nouns chattering (also a noun for a flock of **Magpies**); drum; troubling and vein.

The **Goosander** shares the collective noun of doping with the **Shelduck**.

Collective nouns for the **Goshawk** are shared with the **Sparrowhawk**, a close relative (and the **Raven**) namely aerie from the name of its nest and kettle. In addition the names cast and gross apply to the **Goshawk**. A cast is a term used in falconry to mean the number of birds a falconer releases at a time.

A collective noun for the **Great Spotted Woodpecker**, the **Green Woodpecker** and the **Lesser Spotted Woodpecker** is a descent.

The **Grey Heron**'s collective nouns are hedge; rookery, from the way the bird nests in trees colonially; scattering; sedge and siege.

The collective nouns for the **Grey Partridge** are bew; clutch; covey, jug, from the way a group huddle together with their heads turned outwards and warren.

The **Grey Plover**'s collective nouns include congregation (the same as the **Golden Eagle** and **Golden Plover**) and wing.

The breeding colony of the **Guillemot** is called a loomery. Other nouns include bazaar and raft.

A flock of **House Martins** is called a richness.

The **House Sparrow** has a range of collective nouns, including host; knot; quarrel; tribe and ubiquity.

The **Jackdaw**'s collective nouns include clattering and train.

The close cousin of the Jackdaw, the **Jay**, has band; party and scold as collective nouns.

The **Lapwing** has a range of collective nouns including ascension, perhaps from the way flocks ascend into the sky when disturbed; bevy;

deceit, from the way it deceives predators of its young by feigning injury; desert and exaltation.

A flock of **Linnet** is called a parcel.

Like its Corvid cousins, the **Magpie** enjoys a range of collective nouns, including charm; conventicle, meaning a small, unofficial religious meeting which were banned at one time; gulp; murder, from the birds predatory behaviour; tidings; tittering and tribe.

A collective noun for a flock of **Merlin** is a leash.

A flock of **Moorhen** is called a plump.

A gathering of **Pheasant**s is called a bouquet in flight; covey; head and nide.

The **Quail**'s collective nouns include bevy; covey and drift, names which are used for several other birds.

The **Raven** has a long and varied list of collective nouns including aerie from its lofty nest; building; clamour; congress; conspiracy; horde; murder; unkindness and storytelling. Some reflect its dark character like conspiracy, murder and unkindness.

The **Rock Dove**'s collective nouns include cote, from the name for a building housing the birds; dole; dule; flight; piteousness and prettying.

The **Rook** shares the collective noun parliament with the Owls plus its fellow Corvid the Carrion Crow. In addition the nouns building and clamour refer to the Rook. The largest recorded UK rookery was 6700 nests at Hatton Castle, Aberdeenshire and the largest recorded roost in the UK was 65 000 birds in Scotland.

The **Ruff**'s behaviour at a lek has already been described. In addition the nouns hill and sea apply to the bird.

A flock of **Sanderling** are called a grain.

Predictably a collective noun for the **Skylark** is ascension. Others include bevy (a common collective noun) and exaltation, which is also used for a flock of **Lapwing**.

A flock of **Snipe** is called a walk or a wisp, when flying.

A collective noun for the **Song Thrush** is mutation plus rafter.

The **Sparrowhawk**'s collective nouns include aerie; cast; kettle; mew, from the sound the birds make; moulting and screw.

The spectacular flocking behaviour of the **Starling** has already been mentioned, and the common name for this is a murmuration. Other names include chatter, which the birds do incessantly; scintillation, which their flocking behaviour is and scourge, perhaps for the people that suffer the endless chatter of the birds or the mess they make?

Swallows are seen flocking in the autumn as they prepare for their migratory flight and these are called a flight or a gulp.

In addition to the collective nouns the **Teal** shares with other ducks, the noun spring is also used, based on the way in which a flock of Teal rise directly from the ground or water, without the usual gradual lift off.

The now rare **Turtle Dove** has many collective nouns - bale; cote; dole; dule; flight; nest; pitying; prettying and turn, all nouns it shares with the **Woodpigeon**.

The **Wigeon** shares the collective nouns for ducks generally plus balding; bunch; coil; company; knob and trip.

The **Woodcock** has the collective nouns covey, fall and plump.

The **Wren**'s collective nouns include chime and herd.

MYTH, MAGIC AND FACT

The long and intimate association of humans with birds has given rise to many interesting tales, lore and myths. Some are factual others are mythological but they all reflect how important birds have been and are to human lives in many cultures. Several of these are enshrined in our culture and live on in music, poems, stories, nursery rhymes, paintings, flags, coats of arms and songs. Some, as we have already seen, are incorporated into bird's names.

Individual cultures and epochs have ascribed certain characteristics to individual birds. Across cultures some of these are contradictory. For example, **Owls** in some cultures are described as being wise whilst in others they are evil. This symbolism is powerful in religions and for nations. For example, in Judaism and Christianity the **Dove** is a symbol of peace and life and in the New Testament specifically, a symbol of the Holy Spirit. The symbolism of the Dove has been used by organisations such as the World Peace Congress, to represent peace. Birds have been used in heraldry and many nations have used birds to represent the nature of their nation in their coat of arms. **Eagles** are popular appearing in the coat of arms of countries such as the Czech Republic, Egypt, Ghana, Indonesia and Mexico. National flags incorporating a bird include Albania - Eagle; Dominican Republic - Parrot; Papua New Guinea - Bird of Paradise and Uganda - Red Crowned Crane.

There is a fine line between lore, which has some basis in reality and myths, which are purely fictional. Some folklore started off being believed only later to be proven a myth. We saw that with the **Barnacle Goose**. The prevalent story of how the Goose bred was given folklore status for centuries, being believed by many, but it turned out to be a complete myth! The Goose did not breed under water and emerge from a shell fish! The basis for this story was an attempt to explain where migratory birds went after a season here in Britain. As migration was not a fully established and widely accepted scientific fact until the 19th century other myths abounded, which at the time provided an acceptable explanation. For example, the **Swallow** was said to sink into mud in autumn and rise again the next year. In the 16th century the myth was that they hibernated in mud and fishermen were able to catch and revive them by holding them to a fire. A Royal Society investigation in 1660's confirmed this! Another tale was stated by Gilbert White who wrote in 1771 "..at least many of the swallow kind do not leave us in winter, but lay themselves up like insects or bats, in a torpid state .... as bats do".

In many cultures, such as during the Greek, Roman and Scandinavian epochs, birds were given a wholly mythological status. The authors of the myths took the perceived characteristics of certain birds and used these to make a powerful point in the stories they told. For example, Doves, Owls, Corvids and Eagles appear in many mythological stories in several cultures. For some birds their names derive from these stories. Some of these perceptions still live on today for example, a Dove often represents peace, an Owl wisdom, a Raven evil and an Eagle strength.

Folk lore abounds in many cultures. Given the close association and interaction of humans and birds and, in some instances, the reliance of local people on birds, it is not surprising that there are numerous tales, stories and lore relating to birds. Much of this may well be lost, as the predominantly local tales were passed down orally. However, we still have a rich range of material to draw on. Many people had a strong belief in this lore and some still persist today as superstitions, such as turning over a coin in your pocket on hearing the first **Cuckoo** in spring to bring good luck. Again, many local names and some formal and scientific names derive from this lore. In some instances a lack of knowledge and understanding led to these beliefs, such as the thinking that the **Wren** was the female partner of the **Robin**. It was only when ornithology was established as a scientific discipline and our knowledge and understanding of birds built up that inaccurate stories and lore were corrected.

Many mythological tales and folklore are based on anthropomorphism, which is defined as attributing human characteristics to creatures (in this case, birds). In doing so we impute attributes onto birds which mainly they do not possess. Whilst a Dove is a gentle bird the attribute of peace given to the bird is a human one, not avian. But we still refer to peacemakers as Doves. Wisdom is exclusively a human attribute and Owls do not possess wisdom. Birds possess intelligence which is not the same as wisdom. Corvids, especially Ravens, are highly intelligent, ranking alongside apes in solving logical problems and memory tests. Corvids also display high levels of social behaviour and experiments have concluded that Magpies demonstrate emotions, such as loss and grieving.

However, over the millennia many cultures have used birds symbolically in a major way. Opinions are divided on bird behaviour. One body of opinion believes that birds (like all living organisms) are motivated wholly by the instinct of the individual to survive and reproduce and this is the sole explanation of all their behaviour. So for example, the Dove's gentle behaviour has emerged from the evolutionary process as part of its best means of survival. Others take a different view and argue that bird behaviour is more complex and might derive from motivations other than purely survival. Bird song, it is argued by some, is a pleasurable activity for birds and not purely the biological process of establishing territory and attracting a mate.

Some common mythological stories

This section contains some examples of mythological stories from a range of cultures to illustrate the ways in which the perceived characteristics and behaviour of birds has been portrayed. These stories have been passed down over the centuries to provide the grounding for our cultural beliefs about birds. This can be seen in the use of colloquial phrases, for instance, calling someone a 'wise old owl' derives from ancient, cultural, mythological stories about Owls. Inevitably much of the folk lore was strongly influenced by these older mythological tales. Many local bird names derive from these myths as do a few formal names, scientific names and collective nouns. As a note of caution the exact bird species referred to historically is not always known, so the reference to some birds is generic; i.e. Eagles, Geese, Owls and Woodpeckers are referred to as a group rather than the individual species we know today.

Some of the oldest references to birds come from the Egyptians. From texts and pictures dating to about 2 500 BC the god Horus was depicted as a man with a falcon's head, possibly a Lanner Falcon or **Peregrine**. Horus was the son of Isis, in turn her father was Geb to whom the Goose was sacred. Isis' husband, Osiris, is depicted as a **Heron**, a bird probably well known to the ancient Egyptians. The Romans also identified with birds of prey who gave similar protective powers in times of combat.

The **Heron** appears in Egyptian mythology and is sometimes called the Bennu. One tale is that the bird was self-created and played a role in the creation of the world. It was said to have flown over the waters of Nun that existed before creation, landing on a rock and issuing a call that led to the creation of the world.

The Greek myths frequently incorporate birds in their stories. The aetos dios was a giant **Golden Eagle** which served as Zeus' personal messenger and animal companion. According to some the Eagle was once a mortal king named Periphas, whose virtuous rule was so celebrated that he became honoured like a god. Zeus would have smote him with a thunderbolt, but Apollo intervened transforming the king into an Eagle, setting him beside the throne of Zeus. In other accounts, Zeus adopted the Eagle as his bird when it first appeared to him, before the Titan War, as a good omen. The Eagle was later sent by Zeus to carry the handsome youth Ganymede up to heaven to become the cupbearer of the gods. The bird received a place amongst the stars as the constellation Aquila. Its consort was Lyra, the heavenly Vulture.

This links to the scientific names of the Golden Eagle, the White-tailed Eagle and the Osprey. The Golden Eagle's name is *Aquila chrysaetos* with *Aquila* being an Eagle and the name of the constellation referred to above and *aetos* was the first name of the mythical Eagle of Zeus. The **White-tailed Eagle**'s name is *Haliaeetus albicilla* with eetus linked to aetos again. Finally the **Osprey** was historically confused with Sea Eagles and was given the name *Pandion haliaetus*. Pandion is the mythical Greek king of Attica, with *hali* meaning sea and again *aetus* as Eagle, which we now know to be incorrect.

In another story, Zeus fell in love with the goddess Nemesis but, when she resisted his advances, he turned himself into a **Swan**. Aphrodite pretended to pursue him in the form of an Eagle. Nemesis gave refuge to the escaping Swan, only to find herself tricked into embracing Zeus. To commemorate this successful trick, Zeus placed the images of a Swan and an Eagle in the sky, linking these birds to the constellations Cygnus and Aquila.

The **Eagle** appears in another story. Zeus was angry at Prometheus. Zeus had his servants, Force and Violence, seize Prometheus, take him to the Caucasus Mountains, and chain him to a rock. Here he was tormented day and night by a giant Eagle tearing at his liver. Zeus offered Prometheus two options. He could tell Zeus who the mother of the child was that would dethrone him, or meet two conditions. The first was that an immortal must volunteer to die for Prometheus, and the second was that a mortal must kill the Eagle and unchain him. Eventually, Chiron the Centaur agreed to die for him and Heracles killed the Eagle and unbound him.

The next story explains why **Crows** (or in other versions, Ravens) are black. Coronis, daughter of Phlegyas, was one of Apollo's lovers. While Apollo was away, Coronis, already pregnant with Asclepius, fell in love with Ischys, son of Elatus. A white Crow which Apollo had left to guard her informed him of the affair. Apollo, enraged that the bird had not pecked out Ischys' eyes as soon as he approached Coronis, put a curse on it that scorched its feathers, which is why all Crows are black.

Little Owl

The wisdom attributed to **Owls** derives from Greek mythology. In the story of Athena, the Greek goddess of wisdom, she is often portrayed with an Owl as companion. Athena got fed up with her Crow companion, who was a prankster, and banished it. Impressed with the Owl's wisdom, Athena chooses the **Little Owl**, to be her mascot. The Little Owl was found in places like the Acropolis. Coins were minted with Athena's face on one side, and an Owl on the reverse. Hence the Little Owl's scientific name *Athene noctua*. The story continues with Lilith, the goddess of death, who is flanked by Owls. The rock crevices of the Acropolis were filled with small Owls, believed to be the embodiment of Athena. When the Athenians won the battle of Marathon from the Persians in 490 BC, the warrior goddess Athena assumed the shape of an Owl and led them from above.

Aphrodite was the Olympian goddess of pleasure, joy, beauty, love and procreation. Her sacred animals included the **Sparrow** and the **Dove**. Stories include how she travelled with four white Doves attached to her chariot and Sparrows escorted the carriage. Their chatter and other singing birds announced the goddess's approach with their song.

Several Greek mythological characters are called Cycnus or Cygnus, the latter being the genus name of the **Swan** today. The son of Poseidon is called Cycnus with one account saying that he was rescued as a child by fisherman who saw a Swan fly over at the time. Orpheus was transformed into a Swan after his murder and was placed in the sky next to his lyre, as the constellation Cygnus.

The Greeks also associated this constellation with the tragic story of Phaethon, the son of Helios the sun god. He demanded to ride his father's sun chariot. Phaethon, however, was unable to control the reins, forcing Zeus to destroy the chariot (and Phaethon) with a thunderbolt, causing it to plummet to the earth into the river Eridanus. According to the myth, Phaethon's brother, Cycnus, grieved bitterly and spent many days diving into the river to collect Phaethon's bones to give him a proper burial. The gods were so touched by Cycnus's devotion to his brother that they turned him into a Swan and placed him among the stars.

The final story from Greek mythology involves the **Nightingale** and is the basis for the genus name of the bird, luscinia, meaning to sing a lament and the bird's scientific name *Luscinia megarhynchos*. Philomena was the princess of Athens and the younger of two daughters of Pandion, King of Athens. Her sister, Procne, was the wife of King Tereus of Thrace. Philomela, after being raped and mutilated by her sister's husband, Tereus, obtains her revenge and is transformed into a Nightingale, a bird noted for its song. Procne was also transformed, into a **Swallow**. As a result of the violence associated with the myth, the song of the Nightingale is depicted as a sorrowful lament. It could be that the wrong idea of the female Nightingale singing comes from this tale.

Roman mythology also includes birds in their stories. In one story Proserpine was transported to the underworld against her will by Pluto, god of the underworld, and was allowed to return to her mother Ceres, providing she ate nothing while in the underworld. Ascalpus, however, saw her picking a pomegranate. He was turned into an **Owl**. In Greek and Roman mythology, the Eagle served as Jupiter's personal messenger, and it is said to have carried the youth Ganymede to Olympus, where he served as the gods' cupbearer.

The aquila was the **Eagle** standard of a Roman legion, (another reference to the Golden Eagle's scientific name) carried by a legionnaire known as an aquilifer. One Eagle standard was carried by each legion. The Romans also used to look the bird to decide whether to go to battle, by judging the bird's flight and demeanour 'aves spicere' i.e. to look to the birds. This is the derivation of the word auspicious.

Other Roman tales include one that a dead **Owl** nailed to the door of a house cancelled all the evil that the Owl had caused earlier. To hear the hoot of an Owl predicted imminent death. The deaths of Julius Caesar, Augustus, Commodus Aurelius, and Agrippa apparently were all predicted by an Owl. Owl feathers and internal organs were used in magical potions and pharmaceutical remedies. For example, the ashes of an Owl's feet were an antidote to snakebite, and an Owl's heart placed on the breast of a sleeping woman forced her to tell all her secrets. When a Caesar died he was cremated and an Eagle was sent into the flames to transport the Caesar's soul to heaven.

Stories relating to Minerva, a Roman goddess, are similar to the Greek goddess Athena, both goddesses associating with Owls for wisdom. Minerva, the Roman goddess of wisdom, was the offspring of Jupiter. She sprang from his head, completely armed. She was the virgin goddess of warriors and poetry and her favourite bird was the Owl.

Birds appear in Norse mythology. One of the names given to Odin, the chief god in Norse mythology, is Hrafnagud, the **Raven** god. The tale is that he sent out two Ravens to fly round the world during the day and return at night to report to Hrafnagud what was going on in the world. Hrafnagud translated into the Old English hraefn and thence to Raven. Another Norse mythological tale is of Hræsvelgr a giant who takes an Eagle's form and sits at the end of the world causing the wind to blow when he beats his wings in flight.

Barn Owl

Some common folk lore

This next section contains a range of stories, tales, legends, superstitions and folk lore involving individual birds. Many of these tales reinforce the closeness of birds to humans and how influential they have been in so many cultures. All of them are rich and varied, providing an insight into our relationship with the natural world. Many popular tales relate to weather forecasting, created long before we had weather services. In some instances the weather tale was based on the bird's seasonal appearance, so winter migrants were seen as portents of bad weather, which is to be expected. This section is written in alphabetical order of the bird's formal name for ease of referencing.

Owls have already been mentioned several times in the myths recounted in the previous section. This is a bird whose perceived characteristics are contradictory across various cultures. They are sometimes wise, other times foolish; feared and venerated; despised and admired, with links to birth and death, weather and medicine. Inevitably there are many tales about Owls as a group and the **Barn Owl** specifically. Here are a selection. An Owl screeching at night could lead to a new born child having an unhappy life or it might become a witch. Only Owls can live with ghosts, so if an Owl nests in an empty house, it must be haunted. A tale of stupidity common to many Owls, based on the fact that their large eyes cannot rotate, is that if you walk round and round a tree in which an Owl is perched, the Owl will keep looking at you until it wrings its own neck! In Rome, a dead Owl nailed to a house averted evil. Another Roman myth was that witches changed into Owls and sucked the blood of babies. The association with witches persisted into the Middle Ages, not least because Owls are birds of the dark night and emit loud, frightening calls. Shakespeare referred to Owls in his plays, often connected to evil and death. In Henry VI Henry says to the Duke of Gloucester "the owl shriek'd at thy birth - an evil sign" and is called the "fatal bellman" in Macbeth. In Aesop's tales the Owl is portrayed as being wise. Owl broth was said to cure whooping cough and powdered Owl's egg would improve eye sight.

The **Blackbird** appears in the tale about St Kevin, an Irish monastic saint, which Seamus Heaney wrote about - 'The saint is kneeling, arms stretched out, inside His cell, but the cell is so narrow, so One turned-up palm is out the window, stiff As a crossbeam, when a blackbird lands And lays in it and settles down to nest. Kevin feels the warm eggs, the small breast, the tucked Neat head and claws and , finding himself linked Into the network of eternal life, Is moved to pity: now he must hold his hand Like a branch out in the sun and rain for weeks Until the young are hatched and fledged and flown.'

The lore relating to the **Black-headed Gull** (and this applies to other Gulls as well) states that the souls of drowned sailors become seagulls and hence should not be killed.

The **Black-throated Diver** (along with its close relatives the **Great Northern** and **Red-necked Divers**) are ancient birds with a long traceable history. Over the millennia Divers have not developed to the extent that other birds have and as a family are one of the most rudimentary bird families. The myth is that the birds were involved in the creation of the world. They dived into the water and brought up mud which formed land on earth. This story was prevalent in native North American cultures and also in Finland, Mongolia and Siberia. Divers are also said to wail as they accompany the souls of the dead. The Divers are one of many species of bird that were used to forecast the weather. If a Diver wailed incessantly it foretold rain. A local name for the Red-necked Diver is rain goose.

Rook

The Corvid family is a well known group of birds whose members appear in many myths, tales and lore. **Crows** and **Ravens** in mythology have already been mentioned. Their black colour gives them a dark character, reflected in the collective nouns of murder and mob. In fact, the Carrion Crow tends not to flock, whilst its close relative the Rook does. It is also given the attributes of evil and misfortune. A contrary attribute ascribed to the Carrion Crow is wisdom. Henry David Thoreau, wrote "if men had wings and bore black feathers, few of them would be wise enough to be crows". In fact the Crow family has a proven high level of intelligence (see below).

In another of Aesop's tales the Crow found a bottle with a little water in the bottom, which it could not reach. It found some pebbles which it dropped into the bottle until the water rose high enough for it to drink. Inevitably scientists have carried out experiments to verify the fable and found that the Crow was able to solve the problem as Aesop had written. The Crows had to choose between using solid objects and hollow objects, and they correctly choose the solid. They also had to choose between a jar containing sand and another water, and they correctly chose water. What is remarkable is that Aesop wrote his fables in the 6th century BC (before the time of Aristotle) and attributed the Crow with high intelligence.

In other experiments Crows were given a pairing test. Picture cards were placed over three cups. One card, covering one of the outer cups containing food, matched the card covering the middle cup. A non-matching card covered the other empty outer cup. The Crows learned quickly that the matching card led to food. The experiment was made more sophisticated by using paired cards. Each card had two shapes drawn on it; on some the shapes were the same and on others the shapes were different. Again, if the middle card had two of the same shape, the card on the outer cup with food in had two identical shapes (but a different shape to the middle cup). The Crows were able to select the matching card without any training i.e. it did not learn by trial and error but successfully utilised its prior learning. Another example of corvid intelligence is seen in Japan where Crows place hard-shelled walnuts onto roads and retrieve the opened contents after passing cars have opened the nuts. These experiments show that folk lore about the Crow being intelligent is true even though the authors of the lore were not able to prove it!

Other evidence of the Crow family's intelligence is their ability to use tools. In the wild if a tasty morsel of food is out of reach to the bird's bill it finds and uses a tool e.g. a stick to extract the food. In Japan Crows have learned to crush nuts by placing them on the road at traffic lights for cars to run over them. They have also cleverly learned to 'read' the colour of the traffic lights so they place the nut and retrieve their food on the road whilst the lights are on red!

Chough

The **Chough** is a member of the Corvid family, Corvidae. The bird, once much more numerous and widespread, is associated with the legend of King Arthur. The Cornish version is that King Arthur did not die but his soul was transported into a Chough, with the red bill and legs being red from the blood of battle. According to the same legend, if the Chough re-established as a breeding bird in Cornwall, King Arthur would return. The Chough has now returned to breed there after an absence of several decades. Killing the bird was held to be unlucky. The Chough was not a well-liked bird as it was a thief, Daniel Defoe reporting that it stole not just food but items of cutlery and sometimes took lit candles and set fire to hay stacks and thatch. Thomas Becket, as Archbishop of Canterbury, had three Choughs on his coat of arms, as does the City of Canterbury.

The **Collared Dove**'s scientific name *Streptopelia decaocto* derives from Greek mythology. Decaocto was an overworked, underpaid servant girl. The gods heard her prayers for help and changed her into a Dove so she could escape her misery. The Dove's call still echoes the mournful cries of her former life.

The **Common Crossbill** has been known to humans for a considerable time and its odd shaped bill has made for some tales. One is that the bill acquired this shape as a result of trying to extract the nails from Jesus' cross and the red on the male bird's breast is a stain from His blood. Other tales involve superstitions that the Crossbill could effect cures for colds and rheumatism, that water from which the bird had drunk was a cure for epilepsy and that the body of a dead bird never decayed. A curious set of tales!

Reference was made earlier to the association of the **Cormorant** with Liverpool. It is surprising how much folklore is attached to this. According to popular legend, the two birds (on top of the Liver Building) are a male and female, the female looking out to sea, watching for the seamen to return safely home whilst the male looks towards the city, making sure the City is safe. An alternative version says that the male bird is looking in to watch over and protect the families of the seamen. Local legend also holds that the birds face away from each other because if were they to mate and fly away, the city would cease to exist. An alternative version is that they were designed to watch the city and the sea. Another legend says that if an honest man and a virgin woman were to fall in love in front of the liverbird, the couple of liverbirds would come to life, fly away and Liverpool would cease to exist.

Given how well known the **Cuckoo** is, it is no surprise that there are many tales and lore about the bird. For example, counting the number of 'cuckoos' the bird sings indicates how many years it will be before you marry or the number of children you will have. Another tale is about the bird's arrival predicting the summer weather, as in ' If the Cuckoo comes on a bare bough; keep your hay and sell your cow; if the Cuckoo comes on the blooming May; keep your cow and sell your hay'. In Sussex April 14th is Cuckoo Day and if locals turn their money over they will not want for it. In good British tradition, the Times newspaper prints early reports of the Cuckoo's arrival. A local name for the Cuckoo is gowk, and associates the bird with simple-mindedness. Also the young, newly fledged Cuckoo is called gawky, a term we still use today, often for an uncoordinated, adolescent male.

Gilbert White (of Selborne fame) wrote that the Cuckoo's lifestyle was "a monstrous outrage on maternal affection". This calls into question the earlier point about anthropomorphism and imputing human morals onto birds. The Cuckoo has developed a breeding strategy that works well for them, evidenced by their survival. Their behaviour is amoral and develops on a 'what works' basis not because the bird has any sense of right and wrong. The link to cuckoldry has already been mentioned.

The **Curlew** appears in a 7th century legend. St Beuno dropped his book of sermons in the water off Wales. The Curlew rescued the book and the Saint prayed for the protection of the bird. Hence it is difficult to find the bird's nest.

Understandably the **Golden Eagle** (or some member of the Eagle family) appears in many tales, lore and myths in several cultures. It appears in Greek and Roman mythology (see above). The bird is associated with courage, empire, evil, discord, faith, immortality, power, rapacity and strength.

In the Christian tradition the Eagle represents salvation. It is associated with St John, as the bearer of the word, hence the use of the Eagle on lecterns from which the Bible is read, spreading the gospel round the world. An old legend is that the bird can look at the sun and not be blinded, so can contemplate divine splendour and thus is able to spread light i.e. salvation.

In another piece of folklore there was a race between the **Eagle** and the **Wren** to see which bird could fly the highest. The Wren rode on the Eagle's back and when it had reached its highest point the Wren leapt off and flew higher to win the race. Another race was set up to see which of the two birds could descend the lowest and the Wren won again, by diving down a mouse hole. The Wren was then given the title

'King of the birds. The poet Ted Hughes wrote about this myth - 'The wren is a nervous wreck Since he saw the sun from the back of an eagle. He prefers to creep. If he can't creep He'll whirr trickle-low as his shadow - Brief as a mouse's bounce from safety to safety.'

In golf an Eagle is better than a birdie because it soars higher.

The Eagle appears on many countries coat of arms to symbolise the characteristics the country wants to convey. For example, the coat of arms of Egypt is a Golden Eagle looking left, taken from the Golden Eagle of Saladin founded on Saladin Citadel of Cairo, as has the coats of arms of Iraq and Palestine. The German coat of arms incorporates a black eagle and the Ghanaian contains two Golden Eagles and Iceland one. The coat of arms of Mexico has a Golden Eagle perched upon a cactus devouring a snake. The Moldavian coat of arms has an Eagle holding a cross in its beak and a sceptre and a branch in its claws and the Montenegrin coat represents a two-headed Eagle in flight. The great seal of the United States has a Bald Eagle on it.

One tale about the **Golden Plover** has been referred to already, with the name Plover deriving from the Old French plovier by way of the Latin pluvia, meaning 'to rain'. It is not clear why this bird in particular is associated with rain, although many birds are traditionally associated with the weather in some way. It could be because the Golden Plover arrives in autumn from its northern breeding grounds, (as do many other birds), which is a wet season. The bird's scientific name *Pluvialis* (meaning 'bringing rain') continues the connection. The cry of the bird is said to be the souls of the Jews who were doomed to wander for crucifying Jesus. Another tale is that of the seven whistlers, with six birds calling for the seventh being an augury of death or a variation is that if the six found the seventh the world would come to an end!

The name **Goldfinch** is associated with someone who is wealthy. One tale is that if the first bird a girl saw on St Valentine's day was a Goldfinch, she would marry someone rich. The Goldfinch represents resurrection and fertility, appearing in many old master paintings of Mary and Jesus. The association comes from the legend that its red spot was acquired at the time of Jesus' crucifixion. It flew down over the head of Christ and was taking a thorn from His crown, when it was splashed with a drop of His blood. A similar tale exists to explain the red of the Robin's breast and the Swallow's. In the poem 'Who killed cock Robin' the Goldfinch gave the bride away at the marriage of the Robin and the Wren.

Leonardo da Vinci recorded a folktale that when the Goldfinch is carried into the presence of a sick person, if the sick person is going to die, the bird turns away its head and never looks at them, but if the sick person is to be saved the bird keeps looking at them and is the cause of curing the sickness. Dante wrote that Italian children kept the bird for its health giving properties.

Green Woodpecker

The **Green Woodpecker** is another bird associated with creation. The lore is that when God had finished making the earth He ordered birds to dig out hollows for seas, rivers and lakes. The Woodpecker refused to and as retribution God condemned the bird to peck at wood and to cry for rain, as the bird could not drink from lakes and streams. Connected to this are the local names for the bird including rain bird, weathercock and wet bird, from the belief that the calling bird predicted rain. A Roman myth is that a Woodpecker helped the wolf feed Romulus and Remus. A Roman coin shows two Woodpeckers perched in a sacred fig tree with the wolf feeding the foundling twins.

The Green Woodpecker is in the genus Picus and its scientific name is *Picus viridis* which links to the Roman mythology of a Woodpecker sacred to the god Mars. Picus was widely worshipped and developed into a minor god as an agricultural deity associated particularly with the fertilization of the soil with manure. Other stories made Picus an early king of Italy. In a story by Ovid the witch Circe turns Picus into a Woodpecker when he refuses to be disloyal to his wife

In folklore the **Grey Heron** symbolises fertility, forgetfulness, longevity, morning (as it stands in the water the Heron is first to welcome the dawn), children and regeneration. In Angus, there was a belief that the heron waxes and wanes with the moon i.e. when the moon is full it is plump. Weather-lorists regard the heron flying up and down as a sign of bad weather and flying low as a sign of rain.

The **Grey Partridge** has associations with Greek mythology. The bird's scientific name is *Perdix perdix*, from the Greek perdesthai - a maker of explosive noises. In Greek mythology Perdix was a sister of Daedalus, whose son was turned into a Partridge when his uncle tried to kill him by pushing him off the top of a tower. He flew to safety but avoided heights and re-told his story in a hoarse voice. In fact the bird does not fly high or far, which makes it appealing for shooting sport.

The **Greylag** Goose (often representing geese as a group) appears in the mythology of several cultures. In mythology Geese are associated with the god of fertility, Gula and were the symbol of the Egyptian sun god Ra. The Goose was sacred to the Roman god Aphrodite. Geese gave the famous alarm call as the Gauls attacked the Capitol in Rome and helped the Romans to defend their last stand against the invaders.

The bird's comic waddle and supposed lack of intelligence led to the term 'silly goose'. In Elizabethan times 'goose' was slang for a prostitute and 'goose neck' for the penis. A further tale was that the formation of the geese flight could determine the number of weeks of frost to come. In Celtic culture the Goose was never eaten. In other areas the Goose was eaten as part of festivities underlined by the saying 'If you eat Goose at Michaelmas you will not want for money all year round'. The tradition of drying and pulling a wishbone came from the tradition of eating a Goose at Michaelmas.

The **House Sparrow** has been intimately connected with human activity for millennia. The bird is associated with lechery, because of its alleged public act of copulation, plus lowliness and pugnacity. Chaucer wrote "lecherous as a sparrow". Shakespeare mentioned the Sparrow in Measure for Measure when Lucio complained that "sparrows must not build in house eaves because they are lecherous". In fact the bird is no more lecherous than many other birds. Jesus refers to the Sparrow in Matthew 10:29 ".. are not two sparrows not sold for a farthing; and not one of them will fall to the ground without your Father's will" and later in v 31 "Fear not therefore you are of more value than many sparrows". In the rhyme "Who killed Cock Robin" the Sparrow is the villain with 'Who killed Cock Robin, I, said the Sparrow, with my bow and arrow, I killed Cock Robin'. In Greek mythology the Sparrow was sacred to Aphrodite, the goddess of love and procreation and to the Roman god Venus, the god of love, beauty and fertility. One folk lore is that seeing a House Sparrow on Valentine's Day meant a girl would marry a farmer or marry poor and be happy.

In folk lore the **Jackdaw** signifies conceit, vanity and imitativeness. The bird can be trained to imitate human speech. One item of folklore is that the sight of a Jackdaw by a bride meant the marriage would be a happy one. The Jackdaw appears in Aesop's fable 'The bird in borrowed feathers'. In this tale Jupiter was determined to create a chief amongst birds, and said that on a certain day he would himself choose the most beautiful of them to be king. The Jackdaw, knowing his own ugliness, collected the feathers which had fallen from the wings of other birds and stuck them on his body. When the day arrived the birds stood before Jupiter including the Jackdaw. Jupiter decided to make him king, on account of the beauty of his plumage. The other birds protested and each bird plucked its feathers off the Jackdaw. The Jackdaw was again nothing but a Jackdaw. The moral of the story: 'Hope not to succeed in borrowed plumes.'

Another piece of folklore includes a tale that a Jackdaw on the roof predicts a new arrival, a Jackdaw settling on the roof of a house or flying down a chimney is an omen of death; and coming across one is considered a bad omen.

The **Kingfisher** appears in Greek mythology. As noted earlier the second word of the scientific name of *Alcedo atthis* is the name of a

young woman friend of the Greek poet Sappho. The bird is also a key part of the mythological story of Ceyx. Ceyx was drowned by Zeus and his wife Alcyone visited him in a dream. Grief stricken, she wandered down to the shore. At the same time, the waves carried Ceyx's body to her. She threw herself into the water but the gods, seeing her terrible grief, lifted her up and turned the couple into Kingfishers - halcyon birds, who mate each year at the start of winter. The female halcyon bird builds a nest of fish bones that floats on the sea, and she tends the nest for fourteen days either side of the winter solstice. During this time, Aeolus keeps the winds away and the waters calm, so that his grandchildren are kept safe, hence halcyon days.

Another Greek myth relates to Alkyoneus, the eldest of the Thrakian giants. Herakles encountered the giant during his travels, disabling him with blows as he was sleeping. The hero then dragged the wounded giant beyond Pallene to die. Alkyoneus' seven mourning daughters were transformed into a flock of Kingfishers.

The tale of the bird's striking turquoise and orange colours is that Noah sent out a **Dove** and a **Kingfisher** from the ark and the latter bird flew so high that it was stained with the colours of the sun and sky. Another myth associated with the Flood is that the survivors of the Flood did not have any fire so the Kingfisher was sent to steal a burning brand from the gods. The bird removed the brand but scorched his chest orange. He dropped the brand and the creator threw the brand back at the bird and burnt his rump orange. There are several tales relating to hanging up the body of a dead Kingfisher. In Greek mythology this would ward off a lightning attack from Zeus. In Britain the hung bird would swing in the direction of the wind, whereas a similar tale in France, with the bird named vire-vent (turn in the wind). Shakespeare also refers to this belief in King Lear - "Bring oil to fire, snow to their colder moods; Renege, affirm, and turn their halcyon beaks; With every gale and vary of their masters". In the 12th century a dead Kingfisher hung in clothes acted as a moth repellent. Also a 13th century lore is that 'It is remarkable that these little birds if preserved in a dry place never decay, ... if they are hung by their beaks change their plumage each year, as if they were restored to life', a tale which persisted into the 18th century.

The **Knot's** scientific name *Calidris canutus* associates the bird with King Canute. Observing the Knot feeding on the seashore taught the King a lesson about the limits of his power as King. The bird scurries around the edge of the waves and moves as the tide comes in. The tale is possibly based on the 10th century King getting his feet wet, having commanded the tide to go back. His flattering courtiers claimed he was 'So great, he could command the tides of the sea to go back'. The King learned that 'Let all men know how empty and worthless is the power of kings. For there is none worthy of the name but God, whom heaven, earth and sea obey'. Observing the Knot retreat from the incoming waves helped the King learn this lesson.

The **Lapwing** has the reputation of being a treacherous bird, as quoted by Chaucer "The false lapwynge, ful of trecherye" and Caxton "a foul and

villanous bird". This is probably based on the bird's behaviour of feigning injury if a predator approaches. This links to the collective noun for the bird of deceit. Lapwing chicks were held to be precocious and ran around soon after hatching with shell still on their heads when egg thieves disturbed them, giving rise to brash people being likened to 'lapwings with shell on their heads', quoted by both Johnson and Shakespeare. A piece of folk lore is that the Lapwing mocked Christ at the cross and was condemned to live homeless and call sorrowfully from its wanderings.

Reference has already been made to the high esteem that the wise Little Owl was accorded by the Greek goddess Athene. In contrast the Greeks held the **Long-eared Owl** in low esteem as it was seen as a stupid Owl. From this era came the myth that bird was so stupid it could wring its own neck, which persisted for many centuries. The Long-eared Owl's scientific name *Asio otus* links it to Otus the son of Poseidon, the Greek god of the sea. He was renowned for his strength and daring, but was seen as a simpleton.

The **Magpie** has associated closely with humans and through this has acquired the characteristics of garrulity, mischievousness and noisiness. It is quite easy to see how the Magpie got this reputation. Folklore about the bird includes the saying that the chattering of a Magpie predicts the arrival of a stranger. The Magpie was thought to be a great thief, and it was popularly supposed that if its tongue were split into two with silver it could talk like a man. The Magpie's hoarse cry indicated disaster and misfortune. If the bird builds her nest at the top of a tree the summer will be dry; if on the lower branches, the summer will be wet. No one liked to see a Magpie when starting on a journey but in certain parts of Wales, if the Magpie flew from left to right it foretold good luck; in other parts if seen at all it was considered a sign of bad luck. Another superstition was that if you saw a Magpie you should take your hat off, spit in the direction of the bird and say 'devil, devil I defy you'! Another is when a Magpie was seen stationary on a tree, if it flew to the left, bad luck would follow; if to the right, good luck. In the Middle Ages Magpies were housed with poultry so they could raise the alarm if there were any intruders. A well-known poem casts the Magpie in a prophetic role - 'One for sorrow, two for joy, three for a girl, four for a boy, five for silver, six for gold, seven for a secret, never to be told'. A myth is that the Magpie refused to go into Noah's ark. It perched outside and watched the floods and, because they were enjoying the sight of bad fortune, you should turn your back on a Magpie. Boris Pasternak in Doctor Zhivago related the lore that when Magpies are seen they are portents of snow or there will be news via a guest or a letter.

The **Mute Swan** appears in many tales and myths and represents beauty, grace, haughtiness and death. The scientific name *Cygnus olor* comes from the mythical story of Cycnus who was the son of Poseidon. In one tale his mother abandoned him on the seashore, but he was rescued by fishermen who named him Cycnus, swan, because they saw a Swan flying over him. In another account, he was said to have had womanly white skin and fair hair, which was why he received a name that meant 'swan'. In another tale Cycnus fought in the Trojan War and was killed by Achilles. He was transformed into a Swan after death. A myth about Zeus and the Swan was recounted earlier in 'Some mythological tales'. Several cultures have the belief that Swans transport the souls of the dead to their final resting place. In the Buddhist tradition the Swan represents the same characteristics as the Dove does in Jewish and Christian cultures. In the creation myths of some indigenous American peoples, Swans played a role in creation.

The **Nightingale** inevitably is the basis for many tales and myths because of its distinctive song. The birds represents sorrow or forlorn love in poems, as the song is characterised as a lament. This idea derives from the Greek mythological story recounted in the previous section. In folklore the Nightingale represents happiness and sweetness as well as forlorness and unrequited love. One tale suggests the bird presses its breast against a thorn when it sings, afraid that if it falls asleep it will be devoured by a serpent. Shakespeare used this in 'The rape of Lucrece' - "and whiles against a thorn thou bear'st thy part; To keep thy sharp woes waking, wretched I; To imitate thee well, against my heart; will fix a sharp knife". A variation is that the bird borrowed the eyes of a serpent and refused to return them and the serpent is always trying to steal them back.

In the 12th century the poem 'The Owl and the Nightingale' a furious debate is heard between an Owl and a Nightingale, in which they exchange insults. The Nightingale shames the Owl for the screeches and shrieks she produces, and equates her active time of night with vices and hatred. The Owl in turn replies that the Nightingale's continuous noise is excessive and boring. The Nightingale replies that the song of the Owl brings unwanted gloom, while her own is joyous and reflects the beauty of the world. The Owl is quick to reply that Nightingales only sing in summer, when men's minds are filled with lechery and that singing is the Nightingale's only talent. Finally the Wren intervenes and stops them slinging insults at each other!

The **Nightingale** is the topic of one of Aesop's fables - 'The Hawk and the Nightingale'. A Nightingale, sitting high in an oak tree, was seen by a Hawk, who made a swoop down, and seized him. The Nightingale pleaded with the Hawk to let him go, saying that he was not big enough to satisfy the hunger of a Hawk, who ought to pursue the larger birds. The Hawk said: "I should indeed have lost my senses if I should let go food ready to my hand, for the sake of pursuing birds which are not yet even within sight." The moral of the story is: 'A bird in the hand is worth two in the bush.'

The **Nightingale** was the subject of the first ever live outdoor broadcast. Beatrice Harrison was a leading cellist of her generation. She had the habit of playing her cello in the wooded garden of her cottage in Oxted, Surrey. One evening in 1923 a Nightingale joined in with her playing. Eventually a broadcast of the cello-Nightingale duet was made in 1924 on live radio.

There is an intriguing myth surrounding the **Nightjar**'s scientific name. The myth that surrounds this bird is a tale that was believed for many centuries. Goat herdsmen reported that their goats produced far less milk after spending the night on high ground. Their excuse was that a night flying bird was secretly sucking the milk from the nannies udders. The alleged culprit was the Nightjar. Thomas Elyot wrote in the 16th century "birds like to gulls which appear not by day, but in the night they come into the goat pens and do suck the goats whereby the udders of them be mortified". The name *Caprimulgus* is comprised of *capri* for goat and *mulgus* for milk. So the myth has been incorporated into its Latin name. The real reason for the low milk yield at night is that the goats are feeding on poorer upland pasture at night.

The **Osprey**'s scientific name *Pandion haliaetus* links this bird to the Greek mythological king, Pandion. Pandion appears in the myth linked to the Nightingale, as he is the father of Philomena who is transformed into a Nightingale.

The **Partridge** appears in Aesop's fable 'The Partridge and the Fowler'. A fowler caught a Partridge, and was about to kill him. The Partridge pleaded for him to spare his life, saying: "Pray, master, permit me to live, and I will entice many Partridges to you in recompense for your mercy to me." The Fowler replied: "I shall now with the less scruple take your life, because you are willing to save it at the cost of betraying your friends and relations;" so he twisted his neck and put him in his bag with his other game. The moral of the story: 'Those who would sacrifice their friends to save themselves from harm are not entitled to mercy.'

The **Raven** appears in many tales and myths over many centuries from different cultures. The Raven is one of the most widespread birds, living at low and high altitudes and across most continents. The derivation of the name Raven from Norwegian mythology was described earlier. The bird appears in the Bible a number of times. In Genesis "At the end of the 40 days Noah ... sent forth a raven". Job asked "Who provides food for the raven when its young cry out to God and wander about for lack of food?" Elijah commanded the Ravens to feed Ahab and the Ravens brought him bread and meat. In the Qur'an's version of the story of Cain and Abel, the two sons of Adam, a Raven is mentioned as the creature who taught Cain how to bury his murdered brother. The Raven has a prominent role in the mythologies of the indigenous peoples of the Pacific Northwest. In their mythology the Raven is the creator of the world, but it is also considered a trickster god. In folklore the bird represents cruelty, death, falsehood and the soul of a wicked person. Shakespeare wrote in Othello "as doth the raven, o'er the infected house, boding to all". A native North American story is that the Raven became black after rescuing the moon, sun and stars from and owl's lair.

The **Raven** appears in one of Aesop's fables - 'The Raven and the Swan'. A Raven saw a Swan and wanted to gain the same beautiful plumage. Assuming that his splendid white colour arose from washing in the water in which he swam, the Raven flew to some lakes and pools. But cleaning his feathers as often as he would, he could not change their colour, but through lack of food he perished. The moral of the story is: 'Change of habit cannot alter nature.'

Ravens are closely associated with the Tower of London. According to legend England will fall if the Ravens of the Tower of London are removed. It is thought that there have been at least six Ravens in residence at the Tower for centuries. References place them near the monument commemorating those beheaded at the Tower. This strongly suggests that the Ravens, which were notorious for gathering at gallows, were originally used to dramatize tales of imprisonment and execution at the Tower told by the Yeomen Warders. During the Second World War, most of the Tower's Ravens perished through shock during bombing raids. Before the Tower reopened to the public in January 1946, care was taken to ensure that a new set of Ravens was in place.

The **Red Kite** was a very numerous bird in cities in the middle ages. The bird is associated with cowardice and baseness. In Roman times the bird was reported as taking hair from a man's head for its nest. Shakespeare mentioned this in The Winter's Tale - "My traffic is sheets; when the kite builds, look to lesser linen". He used the Kite's name as a reproach e.g. "detested kite" (Lear) and "you kite" (Anthony and Cleopatra) and "I should have fatted all the region kites with this slave's offal" (Hamlet) and he knew that the Kite took fowl "To guard the chicken from a hungry kite" (Henry VI). Clearly a well known bird in those times!

Tales relating to the **Robin** are many, some having been referred to

earlier, such as the folk tale of the Robin and the Wren. Several tales exist about how the Robin acquired its red breast. One is that it was singed taking water to sinners in hell and another is that when Jesus was on his way to Calvary, the Robin picked a thorn from His crown and the blood spurted onto the Robin. This gave the Robin a protected status and led to the legend that if a Robin is harmed it will have evil consequences. Another Welsh lore is 'Whoever robs a Robin's nest shall go to hell'. Sometimes the Robin is seen as the bringer of fire - along with the Swallow and Goldfinch.

A Thrush (assume it is a **Song** Thrush) appears in one Aesop's fables (The Thrush and the Swallow) that tells of migration long before it was fully accepted. A young Thrush, who lived in an orchard became friends with a Swallow. The Swallow would every now and then come and visit the Thrush. The Thrush would welcome him with his cheerful note. "O mother!" he said to his parent, "never had creature such a friend as I have in this Swallow."—"Nor ever any mother," replied the parent-bird, "such a silly son as I have. Long before the approach of winter, your friend will have left you; and while you sit shivering on a leafless bough he will be sporting under sunny skies hundreds of miles away."

One piece of folklore involving the **Storm Petrel** is that the birds are the spirits of skippers who have ill-treated their crew. Another that they are the damned souls of mariners.

The **Skylark** symbolises cheerfulness, recklessness and song. In times past the word Lark was used generically which might include other Larks or Pipits, all of which are very similar. The Skylark has been the subject of many poems, songs and music for centuries. Perhaps the most famous is Ralph Vaughan Williams' orchestral work, The Lark

Ascending. George Meredith, a Victorian poet, wrote a long poem called 'The Lark ascending' which includes the words "He rises and begins to round; He drops the silver chain of sound; Of many links without a break; In chirrup, whistle slur and shake; All intervolved and spreading wide; Like water dimples down a tide..."; such an accurate and beautiful description of the Skylark's iconic song. Shelley wrote 'To a skylark' Hail to thee, blithe spirit! Bird though never wert, That from heaven, or near it, Pourest thy full heart In profane strains of unpremeditated art. Higher still and higher from the earth thou springest Like a cloud of fire; The blue deep though wingest, And singing still dost soar, and ever soaring singest.'

The Lark is the subject of one of Aesop's fables - 'The Lark and her Young Ones'. A Lark had made her nest in the young green wheat. The

brood had almost grown, when the owner of the field, said: "I must send to all my neighbours to help me with my harvest." One of the young Larks heard him, and asked his mother where they should move for safety. "There is no occasion to move yet, my son," she replied. The owner of the field came a few days later, and said: "I will come myself to-morrow, and will get in the harvest." Then the Lark said to her brood: "It is time now to be off—he no longer trusts to his friends, but will reap the field himself." The moral of the story is 'Self-help is the best help.'

The **Song Thrush**'s scientific name *Turdus philomelos* comes from the Greek mythological tale involving Philomena, hence *philomelos*, which derives from philos for lover and melos, song. This tale was recounted in the earlier section 'Some common mythological stories'. To avoid confusion it should be noted there is a separate species of bird called a Thrush Nightingale (*Luscinia luscinia*), a close relative of the Nightingale, which is a rare visitor to Britain.

The **Swallow** appears in many tales and lore. One story places them at the crucifixion of Jesus, either trying to distract those sent to arrest Jesus in the garden or comfort Jesus on the cross. They are mentioned in the Qur'an attacking Abraha, the pagan king of Yemen who was attacking Mecca. The tiny birds hurled small stones and forced Abraha's mighty army to retreat i.e. when God orders the smallest of His creations, miracles can happen. Other superstitions are that a broth made of crushed Swallow was said to be a remedy for epilepsy and stammering being sympathetic magic, as the bird has a stuttering flight song. Having a Swallow nesting on your house is a sign of good luck but if they abandon their nests it brings bad luck. A special stone from the bird's nest could restore sight. A northern myth was that harming the bird would lead to cows giving bloody milk or that hens would stop laying eggs. A legend is that the Swallow carried fire to earth giving it its red breast.

The **Swift** is very much a bird of ill-omen and many of its local names are associated with the devil such as devil's bitch; devil's squeaker; devil swallow; devilton; skeer devil and swing devil. The association with the devil comes from its screech, which is often heard as small flocks fly around our towns.

In common with other Owls, the **Tawny Owl** appears in tales from many cultures. These are often generic references to Owls as a group rather than a particular species. Tawny Owls are often pictured as wise but are also associated with death and misfortune, from their nocturnal habit and screeching noises. In Greece Owls were associated with wisdom, but the Romans saw Owls as omens of impending disaster. Hearing the hoot of an Owl indicated an imminent death, including that of the Caesars. Shakespeare used this in Julius Caesar "And yesterday the bird of night did sit; Even at noon-day upon the market-place; Hooting and shrieking." The sight of an Owl was a sign of defeat. They believed that a dream of an Owl could be an omen of shipwreck for sailors and of being robbed. To ward off the evil caused by an Owl, it was believed that the offending Owl should be killed and nailed to the door of the affected house. This practice spread across Europe and was still observed by English farmers up to the 18th century to protect their livestock.

The **Tawny Owl** is the topic of one of Aesop's fables - 'The Owl and the Grasshopper'. An Owl, who was sitting in a hollow tree, dozing away a summer's afternoon, was disturbed by a singing Grasshopper. Far from keeping quiet, or moving away at the request of the Owl, the Grasshopper sang all the more, and called her an old blinker, that only came out at night when all honest people had gone to bed. The Owl waited in silence for a time, and then addressed the Grasshopper: "Well, my dear, if one cannot be allowed to sleep, it is something to be kept awake by such a pleasant voice. And now I think of it, I have a bottle of delicious nectar. If you will come up, you shall have a drop." The silly Grasshopper came hopping up to the Owl, who at once caught and killed him, and finished her nap in comfort. The moral of the story is 'Flattery is not a proof of admiration'.

Wisdom is ascribed to the bird in the well known poem published in 1875 in Punch - "There was an owl liv'd in an oak; The more he heard, the less he spoke; The less he spoke, the more he heard; O, if men were all like that wise bird". Horace, a Roman poet, wrote that Owl's feathers were an ingredient for a love potion. Like other Owls, there is often an association with dark magic the Owl being a witch's familiar or the old woman of the night. The Tawny Owl is often seen as an omen of bad luck. A Welsh superstition is that if an Owl is heard amongst houses then an unmarried girl has lost her virginity.

The **Dove** is one of the most frequently mentioned birds across all millennia and in many cultures. The **Turtle Dove** is often mentioned specifically but references might be to other Doves and Pigeons. The bird has been used figuratively as a symbol of peace and life and many artists and writers have used this symbolism. In Christianity the Dove is a symbol of the Holy Spirit, with the Matthew writing "And when Jesus was baptised ... He saw the Spirit of God descending like a dove...". It was also sent out of the ark twice by Noah "At the end of the 40 days Noah ... sent forth a dove but the dove found no resting place " then later "... the dove came back to him in the evening, and lo, in her mouth a freshly picked olive leaf". The Turtle Dove was chosen by Abraham for a burnt offering and later the Jews were told "But if he cannot afford a lamb, then he shall bring ... two turtledoves, one for a sin offering and one for a burnt offering". In the Song of Solomon the writer clearly was an astute observer of birds, stating the Turtle Dove was the sound of the promise of spring "For lo, the winter is past, and the rain is over --- the time for the singing of birds is come, and the voice of the turtle is heard in our land". The Turtle Dove is the only migrant Dove (or Pigeon) in Europe. In Islam, Doves are respected and favoured because they are believed to have assisted the prophet of Islam, Muhammad in distracting his enemies outside the cave of Thaw'r in the great Hijra. From the Russian culture, Turgenev wrote in one of his short stories, Bezhin Lea, that a Dove took the soul of a good person up to heaven.

The Dove is a symbol of enduring love and fidelity, which fully reflects the birds behaviour. Pliny (79 AD) wrote "their chastity is extreme, and adultery is unknown amongst them; although they live together with others, they do not break their marriage bond". Chaucer in 1380 wrote about their fidelity in the Parliament of Fowls "the wedded turtle-dove, with her faithful heart". Shakespeare wrote in Henry VI "Like a pair of loving turtle doves; that could not live asunder day or night" and in Winter's Tale "Your hand, my Perdita, so turtles pair; That never mean to part". Buddy Holly also referred to them in 'That'll be the day' – "giving him all her lovin' and all her turtle dovin'". Two Turtle Doves appear in the Twelve days of Christmas. Finally, Mendelssohn wrote about the Turtle Dove in his anthem 'Oh for the wings of a Dove' which became famous through a recording made by Ernest Lough in 1927. The words come from Psalm 55 "O for the wings, for the wings of a dove! Far away, far away would I rove! In the wilderness build me a nest, and remain there for ever at rest". Such strong imagery from one bird!

One myth is that the **Woodcock** carried the very small **Goldcrest** (weighing 6 g - compare that to the 2 p coin weighing 7 g!) across the sea as the little bird would not be capable of flying so far. In fact the Goldcrest does fly solo across the North Sea! It was also thought that the Short-eared Owl piloted the Woodcock across the North Sea, as they both migrate at about the same time.

Tales involving the **Wren** have already been referred to, specifically the one that led to its name (meaning hen) as a result of the misconception that the bird was all female! In a Greek myth (recounted earlier) the Wren wins a race against the Eagle to win the title 'King of the birds'. Having won the title deviously the other birds condemned the Wren to seek food in crevices, hence its name as a cave dweller. Its scientific name *Troglodytes troglodytes* i.e. cave dweller derives from this. Another name linked to a mythical tale.

Folklore involving the Wren includes that if a Wren's nest were destroyed this would lead to a house fire or death. If a bride hears a Wren that is lucky. The Wren was associated as the female (wrongly) to the male Robin. Known as 'God's bird' and 'Our lady's hen', harm would come to anyone hurting the bird. However, there is a ritual of hunting Wrens between Christmas and Epiphany. A traditional tale is that the Wren alerted guards to St Stephen's attempted escape leading to the first English martyr. Wren hunts took place on St Stephen's day, 26th December. A Wren was caught, killed and paraded from house to house where feathers from the bird were exchanged for gifts. Wordsworth was charmed by the Wren's song, writing "So sweetly 'mid the gloom the invisible bird; Sang to herself, that there I could have made; my dwelling place, and lived for ever there; To hear such music."

REFERENCES

There are many sources of material on this subject in books and on the internet. Below are listed the main book sources used by the author. This is not a comprehensive list nor a bibliography.

Books specifically related to bird names include:

Lockwood, W.P., 1984. *The Oxford book of British bird names.* Oxford. Oxford University Press.

This book provides a comprehensive dictionary style reference to local names for British birds. Gives lots of information on the source of the name and its derivation. Needs a lot of cross-referencing to compile all the names associated with an individual species. Does not include the vernacular or scientific names.

Greenoak, F., 1997. *British birds their folklore, names and literature.* London. Christopher Helm.

This book covers many popular birds on the British list in great detail, giving a list of their local names along with a wide range of information on the bird's place in history, relating many tales and myths, references in literature plus descriptions of the bird's characteristics and life.

Addison, J., 1998. *Treasury of bird lore.* London. Andre Deutsch.

A book covering forty well known British birds giving a limited range of information on their names and greater detail on our relationship with the birds, relevant folklore and many quotes from literature.

Rhodes, C., 2014. *An unkindness of Ravens.* London. Michael O'Mara Books.

This book covers collective nouns for people and animals as well as birds. It provides a detailed description of the derivation of the collective nouns for many of our British birds.

Jackson, C., 1968. *British names of birds.* London. H F Witherby.

A very detailed dictionary style book with entries for 329 birds giving lists of local names.

Kirke Swann, K., 1913. *A dictionary of English and folk-names of British birds.* London. H F Witherby.

A well researched and detailed book listing nearly 5000 local names for British birds. Listed in order of local names, so it is hard to compile all the names for a specific bird.

Lederer, R., 2014. *Latin for bird lovers.* London. Timber Press.

A thorough dictionary style book of 3000 single Latin words that appear in the scientific name for birds. Covers birds worldwide and includes many illustrations and small articles giving interesting extra information about aspects of the life of birds. Does not cover all the British list and the book gives only a few full binomial scientific names for British birds.

Tudge, C., 2008. *Consider the birds.* London. Penguin.

A book covering many aspects of ornithology and is not limited to British birds. Contains a comprehensive section on names and taxonomy for those wanting to understand how birds are classified and a detailed description of the features of the orders and families of birds. Also interesting chapters on various aspects of the lives of birds.

Cocker, M. ed., 2005. *Birds Britannica.* London. Chatto and Windlus.

A monumental work on all aspects of British birds, organised by bird families, with information collected from contributors around the country.

White, G., 1789. *The Natural History and Antiquities of Selborne.*

Gilbert White's 18th century record of the natural history of a Hampshire village, of which he was curate, based mainly on letters to a friend, is one of the first works on ecology. Covers bird as well as many other animals. A fantastic read of a very perceptive man.

Other books on ornithology:

Birkhead, T., 2008. *The wisdom of birds.* London. Bloomsbury.

An in-depth examination of all aspects of a bird's life tracing the historical development of bird science supplemented by some superb illustrations and paintings.

Birkhead, T., 2012. *Bird sense.* London. Bloomsbury.

By the same author, this book provides an in-depth examination of how birds use their senses.

Birkhead, T., 2016. *The most perfect thing: Inside (and outside) a bird's egg.* London. Bloomsbury.

A book that explores in detail all aspects of the fascinating story of a bird's egg, well written with plenty of scientific explanation.

Davies, N., 2015. *Cuckoo - cheating by nature.* London. Bloomsbury.

A well written and detailed account of the natural history of the Cuckoo based on 30 years of research by a leading academic.

Walters, M., 2003. *A concise history of ornithology.* London. Christopher Helm.

A very detailed chronological history of the main players in the world of ornithology. Shows how the science developed over the centuries.

Rothenberg, D., 2005. *Why birds sing?* London. Penguin.

An alternative view of what makes birds sing, suggesting it is not just a survival strategy.

Lack, D. 1953., *The life of the Robin.* London. Pelican.

A seminal work by a famous ornithologist examining the life of the Robin in great detail.

Below are some of the series of titles available on individual birds:

The New Naturalist series published by Collins. Monographs on birds including British Thrushes, Finches, birds of prey and Tits. These books examine the life of the individual species in great detail. Longer length books.

Hamlyn species guides - monographs on birds including Common Tern, Great Tit, Fieldfare, Barn Owl, Kestrel, Swallow and Blackcap. These books examine the life of the individual species in detail. Mid-length books.

Shire Natural History published by Shire Publishing. Monographs on a wide range of British birds. Short length books.

Below are some web useful addresses:

The British Trust for Ornithology - http://www.bto.org/. This site has detailed information on individual species plus a plethora of data from survey work and research. Includes useful identification videos.

The Royal Society for the Protection of Birds - http://www.rspb.org.uk/. Information on bird identification plus survey work and projects.

The British Ornithological Union - http://www.bou.org.uk/. The BOU publishes the official list of British birds (free download). Also carries out detailed research, holds conferences and publishes scientific papers.

Birdguides - http://www.birdguides.com/home/default.asp. The birdwatchers' web-site with news of bird sightings, articles on all aspects of bird watching and ornithology. Some are paid-for services.

Offers a free weekly e-mail news service. Some superb photographs of most British birds.

Most counties have an bird society, whose web-sites contain useful information. They publish annual reports giving detail of the birds seen in that county during the last year, often including papers written by local authors.

Also county or area wildlife societies have web sites with useful information and information on what can be seen where.

Some of the books mentioned are not easy to obtain. A useful web site is Abebooks - http://www.abebooks.co.uk/.

INDEX

A

B

C

D

187

E

F

G

191

P

193

Q

R

195

T

Y

Z

Further copies of this book can be obtained:

1. as an e-book at Amazon Kindle, Apple i-store, Nobu or Kobo. Search for 'British bird names'.

2. as a printed book at Amazon Bookstore. Search for 'British bird names'.

3. as a printed book from the author - contact on:

    a. phone: 01404 813127

    b. e-mail: gdgreen@talktalk.net

who will send one in the post.

Prints of the bird pictures in this book can be obtained by contacting the author - details above.

www.ingramcontent.com/pod-product-compliance
Lightning Source LLC
Chambersburg PA
CBHW050118280326
41933CB00010B/1149